MAKING MUSIC

Copyright © 1992 Merlion Publishing Ltd
First published 1992 by
Merlion Publishing Ltd
2 Bellinger Close
Greenways Business Park
Chippenham
Wiltshire SN15 1BN
UK

Consultant: Denys Darlow F.R.C.M., F.L.C.M.
Designer: Tracy Carrington

Printed in Great Britain by Bath Press Colourbooks, Glasgow

ISBN 1 85737 076 7

Artwork on pages 28—29, 37, 40, 51, 58, 81 and
82 by Jeremy Gower; pages 44, 61, 62, 65, 67, 70,
76, 77, 78, 92, 100, 105, 121, 134, 137, 145
and 159 by Kevin Kimber; pages 8–9, 11, 17, 19,
22, 27, 30, 33, 39, 41, 45, 52, 54–55, 56, 57,
60, 65, 66, 76, 78, 81, 83, 84, 93, 94–95,
98–99, 102–103, 111, 112, 114, 118, 123,
124–125, 127, 132, 135, 138–139, 148–149,
152–153, 161, 163, 179 and 180–181 by Andrew
Midgeley.

Models on pages 91, 97, 107, 125, 133, 135, 143,
147 and 167 by Tracy Carrington and pages 9, 21,
34–35, 43, 51, 52–53, 60 and 74 by Kate Davies.

Photographs on pages 46–47 by Toussain Clarke and
pages 9, 11, 12, 13, 14–15, 16–17, 18–19, 20,
21, 23, 28–29, 33, 34–35, 38–39, 40, 43, 50–51,
52–53, 54, 56, 60, 64, 66–67, 68, 69, 74, 76,
78, 79, 82, 91, 94, 96–97, 98–99, 103,
106–107, 108–109, 113, 117, 119, 120–121,
123, 125, 127, 130–131, 133, 135, 136–137,
138–139, 141, 143, 144, 147, 148–149, 150,
152, 155, 158–159, 160, 163, 164–165, 167,
170–171, 174–175 and 178–178 by Mike
Stannard.

MERLION ARTS LIBRARY

MAKING MUSIC

Written by
Karen Foster
Carole Mahoney
Josephine Paker
Danny Staples

CONTENTS

——————CHAPTER ONE——————

RATTLES, BELLS
AND CHIMING BARS 6
Stamping rhythms 8
Clappers and castanets 10
Shaking the rattle 12
The clash of cymbals 14
Sounding a gong 16
Pots, cans and bottles 18
A scraping sound 20
Plucked percussion 22
Stone chimes 24
Chiming bars 26
Playing the orchestral chiming bars 28
The gamelan orchestra 30
Gamelan music 32
Bells for dancing 34
Striking the bell 36
Playing the hand bells 38
Orchestral percussion 40
Unusual percussion instruments 42
Carnival music 44
Making a steel pan 46

——————CHAPTER TWO——————

MUSIC FROM STRINGS 48
A vibrating string 50
Musical bows 52
Folk fiddles 54
The viol and the violin 56
The family of strings 58

The lyre and the harp 60
Lutes with frets 62
Strumming and plucking 64
The guitar 66
Electric guitars 68
Music on the page 70
The sitar of India 72
The world of zithers 74
Playing the keys 76
The versatile piano 78
Playing together in an orchestra 80
The human voice 82
Singing in groups 84
Listening to opera 86

——————CHAPTER THREE——————

BEATING THE DRUM 88
What is percussion? 90
How do you hear sounds? 92
Different kinds of drums 94
Sounding a drum 96
Rhythm and pulse 98
Talking drums 100
A drum on a frame 102
Friction drums 104
Mirlitons and pellet drums 106
Indian drums 108
Music in the world of Islam 110
Drums for dancing 112
Drums from Japan 114
From kettledrums to timpani 116
Orchestral drums 118

The snare drum 120
The march of military bands 122
Beating the tambourine 124
The modern drum kit 126

──────────CHAPTER FOUR──────────

FLUTES, REEDS AND TRUMPETS 128
Music from thin air 130
Panpipes 132
The didgeridoo 134
Whistles and duct flutes 136
The story of the recorder 138
The modern concert flute 140
Natural trumpets and horns 142
The modern trumpet 144
Modern brass instruments 146
Brass bands 148
Reeds 150
Orchestral reeds 152
Jazz 154
Bagpipes 156
Free reeds 158
Squeeze boxes 160
The organ 162
Electrifying music 164
Unusual wind instruments 166

──────────CHAPTER FIVE──────────

MAKING MUSIC 168
Recording music 170
Going to a concert 172
What every performer needs 174

Learning to play an instrument 176
Writing music 178
Composers' biographies 180
Glossary of instruments 184
Index 188
Acknowledgements 192

— CHAPTER ONE —

RATTLES, BELLS AND CHIMING BARS

From the earliest times, people have always enjoyed making music. This book tells you about some of the thousands of instruments from around the world that are used to make music of all kinds.

In this chapter, you can find out about music made by instruments that are hit or scraped. Many of these instruments were developed from simple, everyday objects that people found in or near their homes. Some of the music played by these instruments is loud, but much of it is soft and gentle. When you look at the pictures, try to imagine the sound that each instrument makes.

There are simple projects for you to try throughout this book. If you follow the instructions, you will be able to make musical instruments with their own special sounds yourself, and then play your own music.

Stamping rhythms

A group of Fijian musicians using stamping sticks

When you stamp your foot on the ground you make a single sound. But when you stamp both feet or bang two stones together and then do it again – and again – you start to build up a repetitive pattern of sounds. This pattern is called a rhythm. Every piece of music needs some kind of rhythm to keep it moving along. And you need an instrument to make that rhythm. When you bang or stamp out a rhythm, you are using your feet as the instrument.

The instruments which are banged, hit together or shaken to make a rhythm are known as percussion instruments. The word 'percussion' means to strike or shake.

Percussion instruments are among the oldest instruments in the world. In fact, we know from looking closely at cave paintings that they were among the only instruments used in prehistoric times.

Fiji. Stamping sticks usually have one closed end which is banged against the ground. The rhythmic sound echoes up into the tube.

Painted tubes

Collect as many tubes as you can to use as your own stamping sticks. You will need to cover one end with tape or cardboard and leave the other end open. Decorate the tubes with bright colours and interesting patterns. Take the tubes outside and bang them rhythmically on different surfaces. How does the sound change? Join up with a friend and combine your rhythms!

Stamping sticks

Percussion instruments, especially simple ones, are still popular today because they create such a strong beat to dance and sing to. In Australia, the Aboriginal people beat hollow sticks on the ground to make an echoing, slightly eerie sound. The sticks are called stamping sticks, and they are also played by people from tropical islands such as

Clappers and castanets

When you clap your hands together in time to music, you are using them as a percussion instrument. But your hands are not the only instruments that can clap! Put a stick, a stone or some other material in each hand. Then bang them together. You've made a hand clapper that you can use to provide a useful background rhythm for many kinds of music.

Ivory hands

Hand clappers have been played for thousands of years by people all over the world. The Ancient Egyptian ivory clappers in the photograph have even been intricately carved in the shape of a pair of hands. Even though these clappers are small – only about 20 centimetres long – they can still be used to make a lively clicking sound.

Egyptian ivory hand clappers

An Aboriginal musician playing wooden clappers

A pair of clappers
made from two
smooth bones

Playing with one hand

A pair of clappers can also be played with one hand. Two smooth bones like the ones in the picture, a pair of small stones or sticks or even a pair of kitchen spoons make simple one-handed clappers. They are held on top of each other in one hand, with the first finger between the two clappers. The thumb controls the top clapper.

The clappers are then banged against each other, the other hand, a knee or any part of the body, using pressure to make them click together.

Castanets

Castanets are the traditional hand clappers used in Spain. They are made from pairs of small, shell-shaped pieces of wood which are hollowed out and shaped to fit into the palm of the hand. A thin cord links the two pieces and is fitted around the thumb. The player then uses the thumb on one side and the fingers on the other side to click the castanets together. Dancers performing the traditional Spanish flamenco dances often play a pair of castanets with each hand. They stamp their feet to the crisp, cracking rhythm of the castanets, while a guitarist plays exciting flamenco dance music.

A flamenco dancer using castanets

A pair of castanets

Shaking the rattle

A modern pair of maracas

A rattle is any hollow container filled with small, rattling objects. Rattles make a softer sound than clappers, but they are just as good for providing rhythm. Traditionally, rattles have been made from round vegetables called gourds which have been hollowed out, dried and filled with seeds. But rattles can also be made of wood, clay, metal or leather. Although many of these follow the traditional gourd shape, they can also be stick-shaped or cup-shaped. North American Indians made stick-shaped rattles by stretching leather over a wooden frame and filling it with dried seeds. These rattles were often decorated with beads and feathers.

An ancient rattle

The metal, U-shaped rattle with a handle that is shown in the picture below is a sistrum. When the sistrum is shaken, metal disks threaded onto crossbars rattle against each other to produce a jingling sound. The sistrum was an important instrument in Ancient Egypt. It was played by priests and priestesses during ceremonies to worship the goddess Isis, and it is also known as the Isis clapper.

An Egyptian sistrum from 850 B.C.

A modern cabaça

South American rattles

The maracas and the cabaça are two types of rattles played in South America. The maracas are two gourds filled with dried seeds. They can be shaken with one hand or two. Many, such as the ones in the picture, are painted in bright colours. Maracas are probably the best-known rattles in the world. You may have had a chance to play them in a school band. The cabaça is a gourd or a wooden cylinder covered with a mesh of steel beads. The beads rattle together when the instrument is shaken. The picture on the opposite page shows a cabaça made from metal and plastic.

Guess what's in the container?

Set up a quiz for your family and friends, using a variety of materials that can rattle in a container. A tin with a lid is ideal, because your materials will make a loud sound inside it. Find some small, hard objects like lentils, dried beans, buttons or rice.

Place a handful of one of your materials into the container and put the lid on. Now shake the tin rhythmically and ask everyone to identify the objects rattling inside and to name the one they think works best. Keep the material that makes everyone's favourite sound and use your tin as a rattle.

The clash of cymbals

These Tibetan musicians are playing cymbals at a New Year ceremony

A cymbal is a round plate usually made from bronze or brass, which is hollowed out in the centre. Cymbals are normally played as a pair. No one knows where cymbals originally came from, although it might have been China, India or the Middle East. Certainly Tibetan monks, like those in the picture, have been using cymbals in their religious ceremonies for hundreds of years. Today, cymbals of many shapes and sizes are played in most countries around the world.

Finger cymbals

Finger cymbals are the smallest type of cymbal. They are attached to the middle finger and thumb with loops of string and are clicked together to play a rhythm. Finger cymbals make an ideal instrument to accompany dancing, because the performers can beat their own rhythm while they dance.

A pair of finger cymbals

A pair of orchestral cymbals

Hand-held cymbals

The large cymbals you can see in the centre of this page are played with two hands. They are held by a leather strap which is wound around each hand, and are held vertically at a distance from each other. The player can make a dramatic ringing sound by clashing the two cymbals together, or a softer, swishing sound by brushing them together in an up-and-down movement. At the end of the 1800s, hand-held cymbals were first introduced into western orchestras. You can read more about orchestras on pages 40 and 41.

Modern cymbals

Today, large single cymbals are often seen as part of drum kits used by rock bands. You can see a drum kit in this picture. Mechanical cymbals are played by pressing on a foot pedal. This raises the top cymbal and then releases it to come clanging down on the lower one. Since the cymbals are operated by foot, the drummer can play as many cymbal clashes as needed and still have both hands free to play the drums.

Cymbal makers

Many of the cymbals produced today are made by an Armenian family firm, called Zildjian, who have been making cymbals since the 1700s. Originally, the Zildjian factory was located in Istanbul, but today it is based in the United States of America. The firm uses a secret mixture of metals and has perfected cymbal making to such a level that it is famous worldwide for instruments that produce a clear tone which vibrates for a long period of time.

A modern drum set

Sounding a gong

A modern gong, part of a western orchestra

Have you ever heard a gong being played? If you have, it was probably a large orchestral gong hanging on a stand, like the one in the picture on the left. Can you imagine what kind of sound an instrument like this makes? A single strike is deep and rich with echoing vibrations that continue for up to a minute.

What is a gong?

A gong is a circular plate made from a mixture of copper and tin. Today's gongs are based on instruments first made in Asia, probably from metal cooking plates. We know that a gong was made in China as early as A.D. 500. Asian gongs play an important part in religious festivals. They have become a sign of wealth. Silver or gold is added to the copper and tin mixture and the gongs are often beautifully carved and mounted on elaborate frames.

Orchestral gongs are struck in the centre to play a specific sound, called a note. This means that, unlike the other percussion instruments we have looked at, gongs are tuned until they have the exact note the maker requires. A gong is tuned by changing the thickness of the metal. All gongs are struck, or sounded, with a wooden mallet covered with felt or wool, called a beater. Try wrapping a cloth around a stick to use as your own homemade beater.

Gong chimes

Gong chimes are sets of pot-shaped gongs mounted in wooden racks. They are found mainly in Indonesia. As many as 12 gongs of different sizes rest on cords inside the frame. Each gong is tuned to play a different note.

A khong wong lek from the Bangkok School of Music and Dance in Thailand

A row of gongs from the Philippines, called a kulintangan

There are many different kinds of gong chimes and their names often depend on the shape of the frame. The row of gong chimes from the Philippines in the picture above are mounted on a straight, low frame. The Javanese bonnang has a similar frame but holds two rows of gongs, not one.

A circular frame

The gong chime in the picture above is the khong wong lek from Thailand. It has a circular wooden frame which the player sits inside. Can you see the large padded beaters the player uses? They make a soft sound. The khong wong lek and the bonnang are played with great skill in the gamelan orchestras, which you can read more about on pages 30–33.

A picture of a decorated Chinese gong

A gong beater

Pots, cans and bottles

Look around your home and collect as many empty glass bottles as you can find. You will need at least eight – but make sure they are the same size and check that nobody needs them! Arrange them in a row and fill the first one almost full of water. Fill the next bottle with slightly less water, and so on until the last bottle has only a small amount of water in it.

Now find a beater. You can use any kind of stick. Start by tapping the first bottle. What kind of sound does it make? Now tap the last bottle. Does it make a different sound? Tap each bottle in turn to play a scale.

Percussion vessels

Each of your bottles is a musical instrument called a percussion vessel.

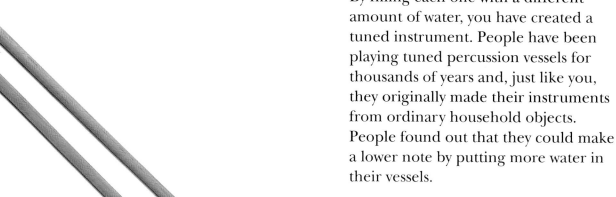

By filling each one with a different amount of water, you have created a tuned instrument. People have been playing tuned percussion vessels for thousands of years and, just like you, they originally made their instruments from ordinary household objects. People found out that they could make a lower note by putting more water in their vessels.

The jalaterang

People used china, tin and glass objects as percussion vessels. The porcelain bowls in this picture make an instrument called a jalaterang, which comes from India. The bowls are filled with different amounts of water and arranged in a semi-circle in front of the player. They are played with thin bamboo sticks to produce beautiful, crystal-clear sounds.

Skilled jalaterang players can produce a quivering note by placing a small wooden spoon into the bowl just after it has been struck. By moving the spoon in and out of the water, they can change the note from a pure one to a quivering one. This note explains the instrument's name – jalaterang means 'water waves'.

An Indian jalaterang

Making music with a glass

Have you ever heard anyone rubbing their finger round the rim of a drinking glass to make a strange, high-pitched sound? If you have, you may not think this noise is very musical, but some composers in the 1800s and 1900s thought it made interesting music.

In the 1760s, the American inventor Benjamin Franklin developed a new instrument from the musical glasses. It consisted of 24 glass bowls of different sizes mounted so that their lower rims dipped into a trough full of water. The bowls were turned mechanically so that the rims stayed wet enough to be played with a finger, just like the drinking glasses. Franklin called his instrument the glass harmonica. The famous Austrian composer Wolfgang Amadeus Mozart even wrote a piece of music for Franklin's new instrument.

Benjamin Franklin's glass harmonica

A scraping sound

Look carefully at the objects on this page. Imagine rubbing your fingers over them. What would they feel like? They would probably feel interesting to touch, because they are all ridged or uneven in some way. They all have a textured surface.

How would you use the texture of objects like these to make musical sounds? You might rub the fir cones together to make a dull, knocking noise. You might scrape the shells together to make a scratching noise. Or you might find a stick to rub against both of them to make sharper sounds.

Wood and bone scrapers

All of these objects have been used at some time to make a kind of musical instrument known as a scraper. People have also copied these natural sounds by carving deep ridges into bone, or animal horns. The ridges make a loud, rasping sound when they are rubbed with a stick. Australian Aborigines make scrapers carved in the shapes of animals and play them with a wooden stick.

A modern scraper

The brightly-coloured wooden tube in the picture is a modern scraper from Mexico. The ridges are rubbed with a stick to make a clicking sound which provides the rhythm for Latin American dance music. Can you see the holes cut into the tube? This lets out the sound that bounces around, or resonates, inside the tube as it is being scraped. Resonators like this hollow scraper make louder and richer sounds than a natural scraper.

A modern scraper from Mexico

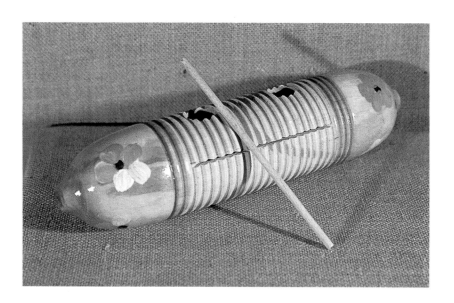

Scraper boards

The metal scraper board in the picture below is called a washboard. Washboards were originally designed for holding dirty clothes while they were rubbed with soap but, like many other household objects, the washboard was adopted as a musical instrument. It was used to play a kind of American music popular in the 1950s called skiffle. Skiffle musicians sing fast-beat folksongs and play guitars and other homemade instruments.

Skiffle players usually hold the washboard across one knee. The player scrapes the board with a metal rod or wears metal caps on each finger to make a loud, rhythmic sound. The washboard in the picture has been specially made so that it can be hung from the musician's neck, which makes it easier to play.

Make a cane scraper

You can make your own scraper from strips of cane. First, ask an adult to help you to cut the cane into lengths of about 20 centimetres. Use some brightly coloured string to tie them tightly together in a line. Then use a stick or a pencil to rub over the top of the canes to play a rhythm. If you put your scraper on top of a box or a bowl, the sound will resonate.

An American washboard player

Plucked percussion

Masai people
playing mbiras

The Masai people of Africa are nomadic,
which means they move around the
country looking for fresh food and
water for their cattle. The Masai people
make music with an instrument ideally
suited to their lifestyle. It is a small set of
metal keys called an mbira, pronounced
'umbira'. It is also known as a sansa or
thumb piano. The mbira is small and
light enough to be easily packed away
and carried when the Masai move on.

The keys of the mbira are usually made
from slivers of bamboo or strips of
metal. Each key is fixed to two wooden
or metal bridges which are attached to a
hollow wood or bamboo block. One end
of each key is left free to vibrate when it
is plucked with the thumb and fingers.
This vibration makes the twanging
sound of mbira music.

A South African
mbira

A modern
jew's harp

You may have seen a modern mouth harp like the one above. This instrument is called a jew's harp. People think that its name comes from the word 'jaw', because of the way it is played. The jew's harp is not often heard today, but in the 1920s it was a popular instrument in certain kinds of jazz band.

Moving your mouth

You can experiment with your mouth as a resonator by using a rubber band stretched between your thumb and first finger. Put the band up to your mouth and twang it with the fingers of your other hand. As you do so, move your mouth to make different shapes with your lips. How does this affect the sound you make? Experiment with your mouth movements until you get the best sound.

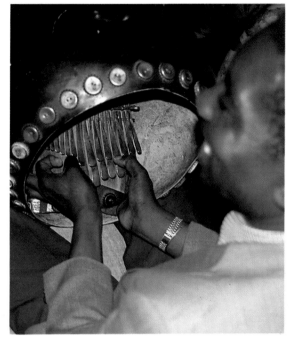

A thumb piano
from Zimbabwe

Improving the sound

Look at the picture above which shows a kind of modern mbira, called a kalimba. You can see that the keys are exactly like those of the mbira, but the kalimba is played inside a hollow gourd. The gourd acts as a resonator. It makes the sound of the plucked keys louder.

Mouth harps

The Balinese musicians in the picture on the right are playing mouth harps. These instruments have one flexible bamboo or metal key. The musicians hold the mouth harps in their mouths and flick the key with a finger. The musicians use their mouths as resonators.

Mouth harp players
from the Bing Gong
Orchestra in Bali

Stone chimes

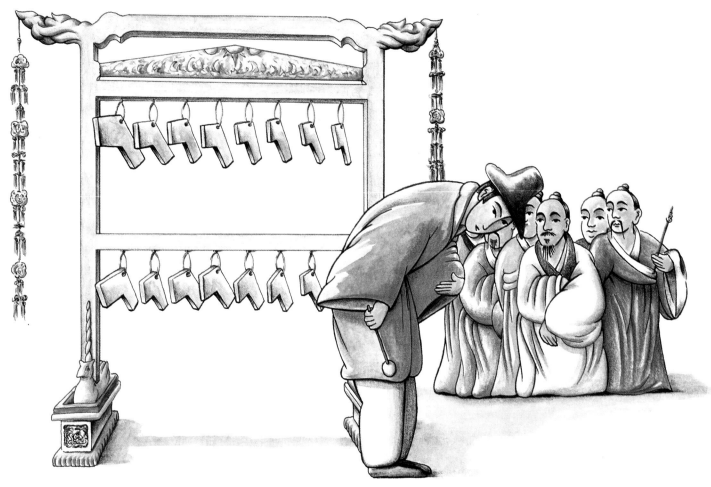

A Chinese
pien ch'ing

'When I smite my musical stone – be it gently or strong,
Then do the fiercest hearts leap for joy, and the chiefs do agree among themselves.'

This verse was written in about 2300 B.C. by a musician named Konei. Konei was court musician to the Chinese Emperor Yao. His verse describes the beautiful music he played on an instrument called a pien ch'ing. Pien ch'ings, like the one in the picture, are formed from two rows of L-shaped stones which are hung from a carved wooden frame. The stones are hung in order of size to make a scale or several scales, the smaller stones making the higher sounds.

Pien ch'ings are still played in China today. You may not think that stones could produce any sound other than a dull thud. But Konei's verse tells you how musical the stones can be if they are played well. They are struck with a soft beater to produce clear, chiming notes.

Volcanic stones

Stone chimes, such as the pien ch'ing, are called lithophones. The stones used to make lithophones are not ordinary stones. Scientists believe that the stones have been affected by volcanic eruptions. They think that the enormous heat from a volcano changes the structure of some kinds of stones. When the stones cool down again, they produce a clear, ringing sound when they are struck. This sound is quite unlike the sound made by any other stone. People may have discovered the musical sound made by these stones by using them as cutting boards or anvils.

English lithophones

Special volcanic stones were found in the Lake District in England, in the early 1900s. Several local people made lithophones by cutting the stones into slabs and arranging them according to size on a wooden frame. The picture above shows one of these simple lithophones.

The huge lithophone below comes from the same part of England and was made at the same time, but you can see that it is a much more complicated instrument. It was made by members of the Richardson family, who also became expert at playing it.

A simple stone lithophone from Keswick, England

The Richardson lithophone from Keswick, England

Chiming bars

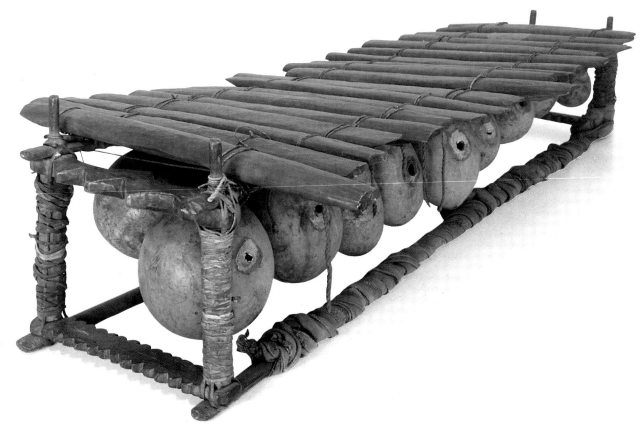

A gourd xylophone
from Sierra Leone

Chimes made from wood and metal are probably more familiar to you than lithophones. Usually, the wood or metal is cut into bars of different sizes and placed on a frame. Wooden chiming bars are called xylophones and metal chiming bars are called metallophones.

Metallophones and xylophones are tuned instruments. Each bar is cut to an exact length and thickness to produce the chosen note accurately. The smallest bars play the highest notes in the scale and the largest bars play the lowest ones. The bars are fixed to the frame in order of size so that the notes build on each other in scales. You can read more about this on pages 28 and 29.

Improving the sound

The large xylophone in the picture above comes from Africa. Can you see the gourds hanging underneath each wooden bar? The largest gourd contains the most air. It is hung beneath the largest and lowest-sounding bar.

The gourds are resonators. The air inside each one strengthens the sound of the note made by the bar above it. Sometimes the gourds have a hole at their base. These holes are covered with the thin web-like material which spiders spin to cover their eggs. When the note is played, this soft material vibrates, adding an interesting buzzing sound to the note.

Marimbas

The spectacular xylophones in the picture above are called marimbas. Marimbas come from Central America. The wooden tubes hanging down underneath them are carved resonators. The marimba is much larger than most xylophones. As you can see, several musicians play it at the same time.

Like other xylophones, it is struck with soft-ended mallets to produce a rich, melodic sound.

Metallophones

Metallophones look similar to xylophones, but they have bars made of copper or steel instead of wood. They are particularly important instruments in the Far East. The beautifully carved metallophone below is called a saron. The carved wooden box is a resonator. In Indonesia, sarons are used to play the main tune, or melody, in special bands called gamelan orchestras. You can read more about these on pages 30–33.

There is another metallophone which is played in the gamelan orchestra. It is called a gender. Unlike the saron, it has a separate bamboo resonator for each bar. The gender produces a softer, more muted sound, which adds to the melody played by the saron.

A marimba band from Guatemala

A saron from Indonesia

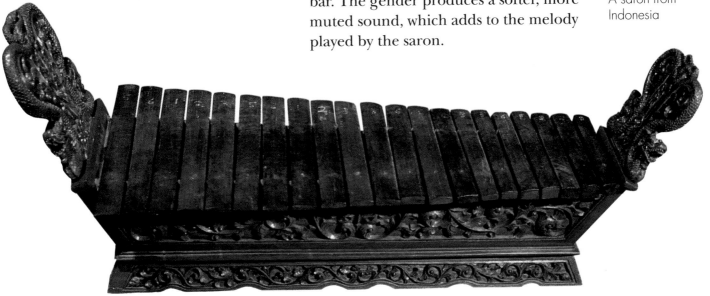

Playing the orchestral chiming bars

The layout of a modern xylophone

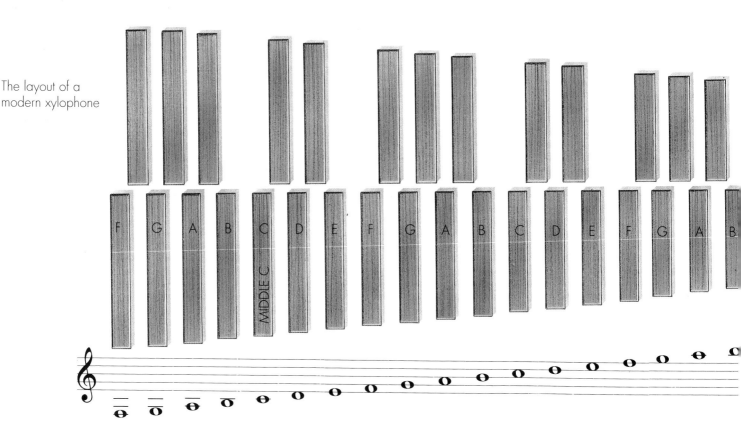

All modern western orchestras include a group of percussion instruments which is known as the percussion section. Chiming bars are an important part of this section. The orchestral xylophone and marimba are just modern versions of the chiming bars we have already looked at. The percussion section also usually includes a metallophone called a glockenspiel.

You play these three instruments with sticks covered at one end with rubber, wood or plastic. You have to use a light touch to make sure your stick bounces quickly off the bar as you strike it. If you let your stick linger on the bar, the note will be muffled rather than clear and true.

Holding your sticks

The chiming bars are played by hitting the bars with the right and left hand alternately. You hold each stick between your thumb and index finger, with your palm pointing downward. You can extend the forefinger to improve the control.

Two ways to hold one stick

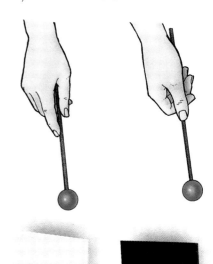

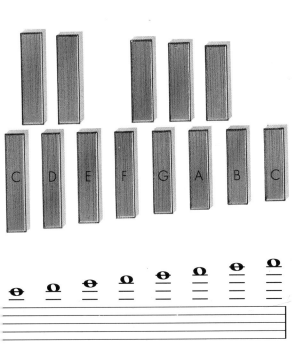

Playing the xylophone

The Scottish percussionist Evelyn Glennie, playing the xylophone

To find out how to play the chiming bars, we can look in detail at the xylophone. The diagram on the left shows how the bars are laid out according to their size. Each bar plays one note. Each note is named after one of the first seven letters of the alphabet: A, B, C, D, E, F and G. Western music is based on a scale of eight notes, which is called an octave. Each octave starts and ends with a note of the same name. One simple octave starts with the note C. Find a C on the diagram. Then find the C which is eight notes, or an octave, higher. This C sounds higher than middle C. We say it has higher pitch.

The xylophone's scales go from F to C. Count the notes. You will see that there are three and a half octaves on the bottom set of bars. All these notes are the main notes. The top set of bars are notes that fall between the main notes. The xylophone player has to watch the instrument and the conductor and read the music – and all of these at the same time!

Look at the photograph of the talented Scottish percussionist Evelyn Glennie on this page. She is using four sticks, two in each hand, to play a xylophone. To hold two sticks in one hand, cross the sticks under your palm with the stick pointing inwards on top. Use your thumb and forefinger to control the movement of the sticks.

Holding two sticks

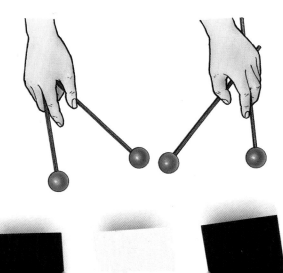

The gamelan orchestra

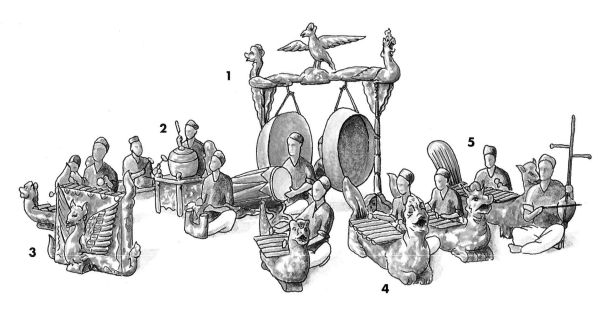

The layout of an average gamelan orchestra

1. gong ageng
2. bonnang
3. gender
4. saron
5. gambang kayu

The picture on the opposite page shows a group of musicians, most of whom are playing percussion instruments. This is a gamelan orchestra, and it is a common sight in Indonesia. Most villages have their own orchestra which plays a central role in village life. The local orchestra, its instruments and its music are the pride of every community.

The instruments

A gamelan orchestra can consist of up to 40 instruments, all of which are usually made from bronze. They can be made from bamboo, which gives a different sound. Because the instruments are always made by a local specialist, each orchestra has a different sound, too.

The arrangement of the instruments is important. There are nine basic types of instruments in the larger gamelans and their position on the stage follows a set pattern. You can see this pattern in the picture above. You will notice that there can be several instruments of each type in one orchestra.

The spirit of the orchestra

The most important instrument is the main gong, or gong ageng. It hangs from a wooden frame and produces a deep, ringing sound when struck. Many believe that the gong ageng is the home of the spirit of the orchestra and people will often pay to get some of the water the instrument has been washed in because they believe it has special powers. The gong chime in the orchestra is called the bonnang. You have already read about this on page 17.

Melodic chiming bars

Xylophones and metallophones are also important gamelan instruments. The main tune, or melody, is played on a metallophone called a saron, while another metallophone, the gender, supports the melody. You have read about these instruments on page 23. The gamelan orchestra also usually contains a xylophone which is called a gambang kayu.

A gamelan orchestra playing at a festival in Bali

Gamelan music

An Indonesian shadow puppet show

Gamelan music is built around a scale of five notes which is often used in eastern music. It is called a pentatonic scale. All the instruments in the gamelan orchestra are tuned to two different pitches, called slendro and pelog. Many orchestras have two sets of all the instruments, one for each pitch. The players switch between the two pitches, but never mix them. Each slendro instrument is placed at a right angle to its pelog partner.

The musicians play from memory. They learn the basic tunes by heart and then add to them as they feel like it, a technique we call improvisation. The music falls into sections, called gongans, each of which finishes with a stroke on the gong ageng. There is a pause, and then the next gongan begins. The musicians are usually so skilled that they amaze their audiences with their playing.

Spiritual music

The gamelan orchestra plays an important part in spiritual life. Its music accompanies religious ceremonies and important events such as weddings. This means that the orchestra itself has a special spiritual meaning for local people. There are many rituals associated with the orchestra. For example, each instrument is thought to have its own character. A musician will never step over an instrument because it would be disrespectful to do so.

Music for entertainment

The gamelan is also an important part of the most exciting form of entertainment in Indonesia – puppet shows. The puppets are made from leather, wood and cloth and are controlled with bamboo sticks. They are moved behind a screen so that lamps throw their shadows onto the screen, just as in the picture at the top of this page. Most performances start in the late evening and continue until dawn.

During a performance, the orchestra is controlled by one person, called the dalang, who is also the puppeteer and narrator. The dalang skillfully moves beautifully decorated puppets, while gamelan music plays.

Two Indonesian puppets

Bells for dancing

An Indian picture, painted in 1850, called *Three Musicians and a Dancing Girl*

The Indian dancer stands completely still. She bends her knees and her legs point outwards from her body. Then she slowly raises one hand and slightly turns one ankle as she begins to dance. She stamps her foot – first her heel and then her toes. She twists her hands and fingers. Her head turns from side to side, and her eyes stare.

Traditional Indian dances are very powerful in their effect. And the sounds the dancer makes help to create the drama. Each time she moves her neck, her wrists, or her ankles, small bells ring. These tiny bells are called jingles. They are worn by dancers so that the sound they make draws attention to every movement, no matter how small it is.

Pellet bells

On its own, one of these small bells would make very little noise, so several are always grouped together to increase the effect. Jingles are also called pellet bells because they have a small pellet inside them. The pellet rattles around against the metal case to make the bell sound.

A jingle from Spain

Morris dancing

In England, there is an energetic type of folk dancing called Morris dancing. Morris dancing is a celebration of good fortune that takes place at special times of the year, especially early spring. The dancers, dressed in white and decorated with brightly coloured ribbons, wear jingles on ribbons around each knee. Some of the dancers carry sticks. As they jump and shout, the bells they wear add to the excitement of this happy dance.

Because jingles are worn by dancers, they are often thought of as jewellery rather than as musical instruments. Jingles became more and more elaborate and were often made of gold or silver, like the Spanish jingle above.

Shells and nuts

Jingles can be made from many kinds of materials. People have used shells and nuts threaded onto thongs as simple instruments for thousands of years. You can make your own jingle jewellery from beads, shells or pasta shapes threaded onto string.

Cut your strings into different lengths before you thread on your chosen jingles. Then you can knot them around your ankles or wrists like an Indian dancer, or around your knees like a Morris dancer.

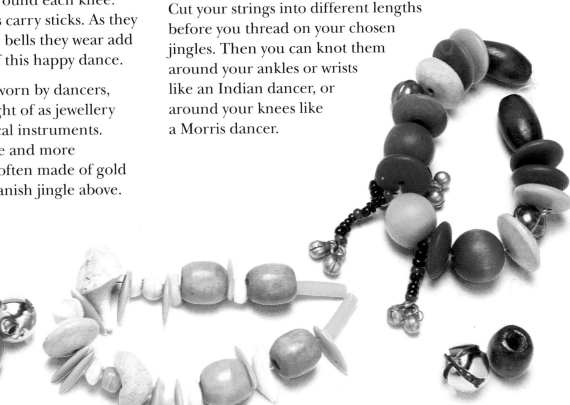

Striking the bell

The enormous Russian bell in the picture below is the heaviest bell in the world. It is called the Czar Kolokol bell and it weighs nearly 200 tons. It was made in 1735, but it was too heavy to be used. It now stands on a large platform in the Kremlin in Moscow. A fragment of the huge bell has broken away and even this piece weighs about 11 tons!

Not all bells are as large as the Kolokol bell, but many are much older. Metal bells dating from 1000 B.C. have been found in the Middle East, in Iran. People in many countries have used the sound made by wooden or metal bells to frighten away enemies and evil spirits. Bells are often used in religious ceremonies and as charms to bring people good fortune.

A picture of the huge Russian Kolokol bell

A Japanese
temple bell

Sounding a bell

All bells need an instrument to strike, or sound, them. They must be struck on the rim, where the metal is thickest, to produce the loudest sound. Each bell makes a different musical note. The larger the bell is, the lower the note. A bell can be struck from the inside or the outside, and the striker can be attached to the bell or can be separate from it.

Temple bells

The picture on the right shows a large Japanese temple bell. It is struck on the outside with a wooden beam pulled by a rope. Bells like this are usually housed in a special building within the grounds of the temple and are rung to call people to prayer.

Clapper bells

Most bells are sounded by an instrument which is attached to the inside of the bell. This is called a clapper. Clappers can be made from several different materials, such as bone or shell, but most are forged from metal. Clappers can be round or square in shape.

Change ringing

In Europe, bell towers are a feature of many churches. The bells are hung high up in the tower and rung in groups of five or more. This is called change ringing, and it is a complicated skill that takes a long time to learn. These pictures show you how it is done.

Each bell is mounted on a wooden wheel, which can be moved by pulling the rope attached to it. Each bell ringer pulls his or her rope down, and the bell swings up on its wheel. He or she pulls down again, and the bell swings down, ringing as it falls. Each bell has a different note and must be rung at just the right time so that the result is an evenly spaced set of sounds, called a peal. As you can imagine, it is crucial that each bell ringer pull down at precisely the right second. This is especially important when the peal gives way to a tune.

1. The bell is in its resting position

2. A series of gentle pulls swings the bell upside down. A brake, or stay, stops it from swinging over the top

3. A sharp pull on the rope swings the bell down. It strikes and then continues up again

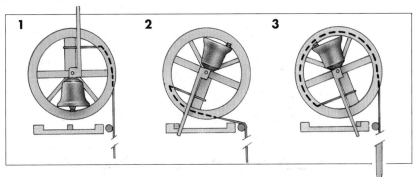

Playing the hand bells

A set of 13 English hand bells

Hand bells are the same shape as the larger church bells, but are small enough to be held in the hand with a leather strap. The bells are made from a special metal called bronze. Inside each bell there is a clapper to hit the sides and create the sound. The clapper is a metal rod with hard leather pads on the end. Below the hand strap there is a leather collar. This prevents the bell from being touched as it rings, since this would spoil the tone.

Tibetan monks playing hand bells during a religious ceremony

Carrying a bell

Hand-held bells have been used throughout the ages to send signals. The sound of a hand bell would announce that the bell ringer had an important message. Messengers would walk the streets ringing a hand bell and shouting news to people walking by. This still happens on special occasions in some European countries, where the messengers are called town criers.

Ringing for pleasure

Today, some people play hand bells just for fun or to entertain others. They hold one bell in each hand and follow written music. The bells are so finely tuned and so light to control that all kinds of music can be played on them.

Each hand bell produces a different musical note, so when a group of eight or more bells ring together, quite complicated music can be played on them. The smaller the hand bell, the higher the pitch of the musical note. The deeper-sounding hand bells are sometimes so large that they have to be played resting on a table.

Hand bells are popular instruments in schools. Many schools have groups of hand bell players, who perform at assemblies and at local events.

A single English hand bell

Orchestral percussion

Look at this diagram of a western orchestra. You can see that each set of instruments has its own place on the stage. Can you see the percussion section? It is right at the back, in the centre. In a large orchestra, there may be three or four percussionists playing a variety of instruments.

Every percussion section has a selection of those instruments which are normally required by composers. They are the timpani (sometimes called the kettledrums), the snare drum, the bass drum, the gong, the cymbals, the xylophone and the glockenspiel.

The composer decides

Some pieces of music are written to include other percussion instruments, too. Some music calls for percussion instruments such as the mbira, tubular bells, triangle and castanets. At some performances, the percussion section can contain as many as 80 instruments!

The triangle

You already know about most of the instruments in the percussion section, but you haven't yet read about the triangle or the tubular bells. You can see from the picture below that a triangle is a thin steel bar bent into the shape of a triangle. One corner is left open. It is played by tapping the outside of the bars with a steel beater to produce a high, pure sound which can be used to resemble bells.

A triangle and beater

A percussionist plays the orchestral tubular bells

The British composer Benjamin Britten

Tubular bells

Tubular bells are formed by hanging two rows of different-length steel tubes from a frame in order of size. The largest tube produces the lowest sound. Can you see how they are played by looking at the picture on the right? They are struck at the top with mallets covered with leather or felt. You can listen to tubular bells in the opera called *The Turn of the Screw*, by the British composer Benjamin Britten.

Playing orchestral percussion

To be a successful percussionist you must be able to play all the instruments in the percussion section. This requires many different skills and may take years to learn. The famous British percussionist James Blades has achieved this, and he is also well known for making and collecting percussion instruments. You could follow his example by making some of the instruments in this book and then learning to play them.

Unusual percussion instruments

A painting of Richard Wagner by the German artist Gemaelde von Schweninsky

This is a painting of the German composer Richard Wagner. Wagner is probably best known for his series of four operas called *The Ring of the Nibelung*. In one of the operas, *The Rhine Gold*, Wagner wrote a scene which uses an anvil as a percussion instrument.

The scene shows Wotan, the chief of the gods, arriving at a cave belonging to a band of dwarfs. The music grows gloomy to reflect the eerie mood of the cave. Slowly the orchestral music dies down, until only one dramatic sound can be heard. It is a slow tapping of metal on metal as one of the dwarfs works at his anvil. The curtain lowers as the tapping echoes around the stage, and the scene ends as the sound dies away.

The anvil is just one of several unusual percussion instruments which composers like Wagner have used to great effect. The percussionist does not use a real anvil to achieve the dramatic sound Wagner's opera demands. Instead, an orchestral anvil made from two or more steel bars is used.

The musical saw

The musical saw is another unusual percussion instrument. It is based on the ordinary carpenter's saw, but it does not have teeth. The blade is held between the player's knees and bent into an S shape. It is played with a cello bow to produce a ghostly, squeaking sound. As you can guess, it is a difficult instrument to play!

An American musical saw player

Tinkling in the wind

Wind chimes create the completely opposite effect from those of the anvil and the musical saw. They are made from small pieces of shell, glass, metal or bamboo, suspended from cords. Wind chimes were originally made in the Far East and hung in temples, where the wind moved them naturally to create a pleasing tinkling sound. They are not often used in the orchestra, but when they are, they are moved by hand.

Make your own wind chimes

First, cut out a circle of thick cardboard, about 10 centimetres in diameter. Make a circle of eight small holes around the edge and one hole in the centre of the circle. Cut nine strings of different lengths and thread one through each hole. Make knots in the top to hold them in place. Now ask an adult to cut some pieces of bamboo or cane for you. Thread one onto each piece of string and make a knot in the end. Hang up your chimes and let the wind move the wood together. Try using stones to make a different sound.

A steel band from
Barbados

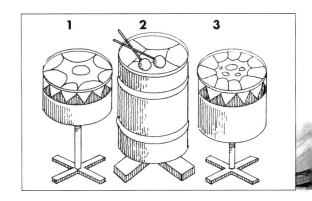

1. A tenor pan
2. A bass pan
3. A guitar pan

Carnival music

You are in a hot, sunny country walking through a busy market, full of bright colours and exotic smells. What kind of music would you like to be listening to? Would it be slow, sad music? No – you would probably want to hear music with a rhythm to match your cheerful mood.

There is one instrument that would produce just the right kind of lively music for these occasions. It is called the steel drum, or pan, and it comes from Trinidad in the West Indies. Carnivals are important events there and people have always joined in the joyful celebrations by banging out a lively rhythm on anything they could find, from biscuit tins to dustbins.

Eventually, someone found that steel oil drums made a rich, musical sound and steel pans are still made from oil drums today.

Different notes

The first steel pan players found they could play different notes by making different-sized bulges in the surface of the pan. Then they cut the main body of the drum to different sizes and found that this gave the notes different tones. You can find out how a steel pan is made by turning to pages 46 and 47.

The steel band

The large picture on the opposite page shows you what a steel band looks like when it is made up of several different-sized steel pans. There are three sections in a steel band. You can see the shape of the pans in each section in the diagram. The smallest pan is called the tenor pan. It produces the highest notes and is used to play the main tune, which we call the melody. The guitar pan is the middle-sized pan. It is used to play the rhythm. The bass pan is the largest pan and it has the deepest notes. It is used to play another, complementary rhythm.

Steel bands can have many members, all playing different variations of the three main kinds of pan. A good steel band can play almost any kind of music, from rock music, reggae and calypso to classical music.

Making a steel pan

Sinking the pan

Tracing the notes

Punching in
the notes

Many steel pan players make their own instruments so that they can be sure that the pan they play has exactly the sound they want. Making a steel pan is a complicated job, with nine main stages.

First, a drum is chosen. If you look back to pages 44 and 45, you will see that there are three types of steel pan. Here, a drum with the right thickness of metal to make a tenor pan is selected.

Now the end of the oil drum is pounded with a heavy leather mallet. It must be pounded into a smooth curve about 20 centimetres deep. This process is called sinking the pan.

Patterns of the notes are traced onto the sunken shape with chalk. The tenor pan has 28 notes, and these have to be marked in a precise way.

Now the shape of each note must be punched into the metal. You can see how this is done using a punch and a hammer to make lots of indentations.

Cutting the pan

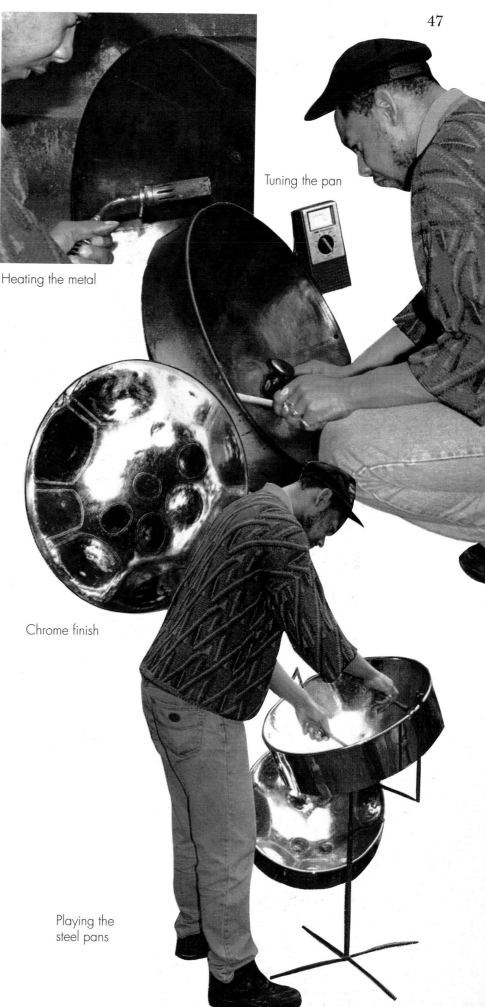

Heating the metal

Tuning the pan

Chrome finish

Playing the
steel pans

The main part of the barrel is now cut
to the right size, using a metal cutter.
The shorter the pan, the higher the
range of notes it will produce. The tenor
pan is cut to about 20 centimetres deep.

Now the surface metal of the pan has to
be heated up quickly. Sometimes the
whole pan is plunged into a bonfire, but
here a blowtorch is being used. Once
the metal cools down again, it is much
softer and easier to mould.

Now comes the most important stage –
tuning. The drum maker taps out the
standard note with a rubber-tipped
beater. Then he taps the soft metal over
and over again on the same spot, using
gentle strokes until the sound of the
note begins to change. He tunes the pan
by ear, checking each note with a
mechanical tuner to make sure it
is accurate.

He does the same on the marked-out
places of each of the 28 notes positioned
around the pan. Now the pan is sent
away to a factory where it is dipped in a
liquid metal called chrome. This gives
the finished pan its bright, shiny look.

Finally, the pan is fixed to its stand. At
last it is ready to play.

— CHAPTER TWO —

MUSIC FROM STRINGS

The instruments in this chapter are all sounded by vibrating strings. The strings are attached in different ways to bodies of many shapes and sizes. The most surprising stringed instrument is perhaps the human voice.

You will see from the pictures in this chapter that there are different ways of playing the strings. It is quite easy to make a sound from a stringed instrument, but to play it well requires a lot of practice.

You can also find out how music is written down, and have fun discovering how stringed instruments are played all around the world.

A vibrating string

A Chinese band playing stringed instruments in Beijing Park

You have probably seen instruments which use strings to make a musical sound many times before. But look carefully at the strings on the instruments in the picture above. They're certainly not made from string! Musical strings can be made from metal, plastic, animal gut and even silk. So how do you make a musical noise with a string?

First, you have to fix the string firmly at both ends so that it is stretched tight. If you stretch a rubber band tightly across the top of an empty jar and pull it toward you, or pluck it, you will see how a sound is made. Watch the rubber band shaking very fast just after you pluck it. This movement is called vibration. A vibration sets the air around the rubber band moving in waves which we call sound waves. The waves carry the twanging sound to your ear. You've made a musical sound!

A double bass

A trough zither

Resonators

A vibrating string does not make much noise by itself. But if you fix the string across the open part of a hollow container, vibrations from the string will echo around inside it. The vibrations set up sounds which are louder and richer. We call hollow containers that increase the volume of sounds 'resonators' because the sound is echoing, or resonating, inside them. Resonators come in many shapes and sizes. The body of this double bass is an enormous resonator and it makes a low sound, while the narrow trough zither produces a much smaller noise.

High or low

To make sounds into music, the strings on a stringed instrument must be tuned to produce a specific pure sound called a note. You can find out more about notes by turning to pages 70 and 71.

Notes can be high or low. Long or loose strings produce low notes and short or tight strings produce high notes. An instrument's strings are usually stretched and fixed to a particular length so that they always sound the same.

To make a string sound higher or lower, you can shorten it by putting a finger or another kind of stop in the way. You can try this out on a rubber-band harp. All you need is a box to act as a resonator and some rubber bands as strings. Stretch the bands around the box and start plucking. Make different notes by using long and short bands, or by stopping the bands with your fingers.

Musical bows

According to a Japanese legend, the sun goddess once had an argument with her brother. In a rage, she shut herself in a cave and the whole world was plunged into darkness. So the other gods came up with a plan that would persuade the sun goddess to come out again. They played wonderful melodies on a musical instrument made from six hunters' bows. One of the goddesses started to dance. The gods yelled and clapped their hands. When the sun goddess heard the noise and music, she was curious. She came out of her cave and light returned to the world.

A single string

Stringed instruments which look like hunting bows still exist in Africa and Asia today. They are called musical bows. You can see from the picture below that a musical bow is simply a single string fastened at each end to a flexible stick. The string can be made to move in several ways. You can pluck it with your fingers or tap it with a stick. Or you can use another, smaller bow to make it sound. The two strings rub together and cause each other to vibrate.

Playing a musical bow

Multiple strings

Several single bows can be joined together and attached to a single resonator to make an instrument which creates several sounds at once. We call this instrument a compound musical bow. Each string on each bow is a different length. In this way, each one produces a different note. These compound musical bows are often heard in the music of Central America, Asia and Africa. Look back to the Japanese picture to see a compound musical bow.

Homemade resonators

You can fix any hollow object to a musical bow to help increase the sound it produces. Round vegetables called gourds are often hollowed out, dried, then cut in half to be used as resonators. Half a coconut shell, a tin can or a cooking pot also makes a good resonator. If you hold the bow in your mouth, like the boy in the picture above, you can even use your mouth as the resonator.

Folk fiddles

Folk fiddles are popular stringed instruments used all over Asia, Africa and Europe. Some folk fiddles look very much like musical bows, but some have up to six strings and look more like violins. A folk fiddle is usually played, or bowed, using another bow with horsehair strings.

There are two basic kinds of folk fiddle – a spike fiddle and a short-necked fiddle. The spike fiddle, as you can see from the picture on the right, has a spike at the bottom. It is held upright, with the spike resting on the floor or on the player's knee – if it is not too sharp! A short-necked fiddle is shown in the picture at the top of the next page. It is held horizontally, with the base of the instrument resting against the player's shoulder or chest.

This Turkish spike fiddle is held vertically

Changing pitch

As you know, if you change the length of a string you will change the sound it makes. The note will be higher or lower. This is called changing the pitch of a note. Pressing a finger on the string so that less of it is able to vibrate is one way of changing the pitch. This is easy on most folk fiddles, which have the strings running over a long, thin board called a fingerboard. When you press, or stop, the string with your finger, it presses the string down on the board, shortening it and creating a higher note. Take your finger away – you are back to the full string vibration again. The note you play is lower.

This Apache Indian tube fiddle from North America is held horizontally

Fiddles for dancing

Music from folk fiddles can be bright and lively – just right for dancing! Many fiddlers from European countries such as Hungary play at amazing speed and with great skill. They learn to play the fiddle by ear and can play the most intricate tunes from memory. The most important musician in the Italian picture below is the folk fiddler who stands in the centre. He is playing for a special dance called the tarantella. This was a well-known dance with a fast rhythm which needed quick, exciting music as its accompaniment. Any fiddler who could keep up as the dance went on and on was always in demand!

This painting, by the Italian artist Pietro Fabris, is called *Tarantella with Posillipo in the Background*

The pegs and the bridge

On every fiddle there is a mechanism for fixing the exact length and tightness of each string. This means that the string always plays the right note – we say that it is in tune. Can you see the pegs at the head of the fiddle on the left? The strings are fastened to the pegs. By turning the pegs very slightly, you can tighten or loosen the strings to give slightly higher or lower notes.

The strings rest on a raised, curved platform called a bridge. The bridge lifts the strings up and prevents the bow from touching the body of the fiddle so that you play a clear, crisp note.

The viol and the violin

Playing the viol

In the 1500s and 1600s, a concert or small musical gathering would probably echo to the melodies created by a stringed instrument called the viol. This is a six-stringed instrument with a gently sloping bridge which made it easy to play several strings at once. As you can see from the picture on the left, the musician sits down to play the viol, resting the instrument on, or between, the knees. The bow is held with the palm facing outwards and is drawn across the strings to produce a soft, delicate sound. Viols have recently regained their old popularity and groups of viol players, called consorts, are getting together to play this special music.

The violin

The violin is a smaller instrument than the viol, but it makes a louder noise. From about 1700 the violin started to replace the viol in Europe and today it is probably the best known of all western orchestral instruments.

This picture of a violin shows all the parts of the instrument. Can you see the fingerboard, the pegs, the strings and the bridge? The small hollow at the base is called a chin rest. The player positions the chin in the hollow and holds up the violin to play it. The two f-shaped holes are called soundholes. They allow the sound that is resonating inside the body of the violin to escape and give a full, rich note.

A modern violin with bow and resin

The Italian violinist
Niccolò Paganini

sound. Those that still exist are highly prized and sell for a great deal of money. We still don't know the secret of Stradivari's success – it was probably a combination of the design, the thickness of the wood and the varnish.

In the 1800s, the Italian violinist Niccolò Paganini revolutionized the technique of violin playing. You can see him playing a violin in the picture. He introduced new, exciting methods of fingering and bowing. He often made up the music as he went along and sometimes used tricks such as putting on a blindfold, or cutting one or two of the strings of his violin and continuing to play on the other two strings. People thought he was insane, but he certainly made an amazing sound!

Improving the sound

What you cannot see are two important parts inside the body of the violin. One is the soundpost, which is a small stick fixed near the bridge, and the other is the bass bar which runs up between the soundholes. These two parts make sure that the vibrations spread throughout the whole body of the instrument.

Some of the most talented modern musicians are violinists. The British violinist Yehudi Menuhin started learning the violin when he was four and was already a brilliant player by the age of seven. He founded a school in England for musically talented children. This picture shows the famous Korean violinist Kyung Wah Chung.

The Korean violinist
Kyung Wah Chung

The bow

The violin bow is a flexible stick with thin strands of horsehair stretched from one end to another. The hair can be tightened by turning a small nut fixed to one end. The hair needs to be coated with a soft, sticky gum called resin to make the string vibrate properly.

The best in the world?

The Italian musician Antonio Stradivari was a great violin maker. The instruments he made are now about 300 years old but they still make a wonderful

The family of strings

A string quintet

The violin may be an important stringed instrument, but it is only one of a family of instruments. The other members are the viola, the cello and the double bass.

These four instruments make a similar sound, each at a different pitch. We call the four pitches treble, alto, tenor and bass. The violin plays the highest pitch – the treble. The viola plays the alto, the cello the tenor and the double bass provides the low bass notes. So when they are played together in a group, the effect is very pleasant.

There is a lot of music written especially for the four instruments of a string quartet. A string quartet consists of two violins, a viola and a cello.

1. violin
2. viola
3. cello
4. double bass

1   2   3   4

Look at the picture on the left. You can see the five instruments that form the slightly larger string quintet. Can you identify the instruments the musicians are playing?

The viola

The viola is just like the violin, but it is slightly larger, so the sound it makes is lower. The mellow sound of the viola is important to the string quartet. It plays the middle notes of the musical picture.

The cello

The cello, whose proper name is the violoncello, produces a wonderful rich sound. It can cover a wider range of notes than any of the other members of the string family. Its large body provides good resonance and its notes are broad and mellow. This makes the cello an ideal instrument to listen to on its own when it is not providing the tenor theme.

The cello is far too big to play under your chin! You sit down with the instrument between your legs and the neck rests on your shoulder. A spike on the base of the cello rests on the floor.

Double bass

The double bass is the largest string instrument. It is about 2 metres tall, and its strings are 108 centimetres long. Travelling around with a double bass is not easy! Some players find it most comfortable to sit on the edge of a high stool when they play. Others, like the famous American jazz musician Charlie Mingus, prefer to stand up. You can see Charlie Mingus playing in the picture on the right.

The American jazz musician Charlie Mingus

The lyre and the harp

There is a legend from Ancient Greece about a man called Orpheus, the son of the Greek god Apollo. Orpheus played an instrument called a lyre.

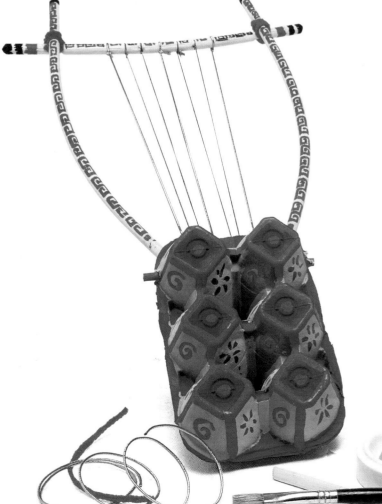

He played it so beautifully that he charmed all the animals with his music.

One day Orpheus's wife Eurydice was bitten by a snake and died. She was taken down into the underworld. In despair, Orpheus took his lyre and went in search of her. On entering the underworld, he was brought before its queen, Persephone. He begged the queen to release his wife and so charmed her with his music that she agreed, on one condition. Orpheus must not turn to look at his wife as he led her back to the outside world. But Orpheus was impatient. Just as he was leaving the underworld he turned round. Instantly Eurydice vanished. Soon after, Orpheus died of grief.

What is a lyre?

The lyre that is mentioned in this sad story is an instrument with strings that stretch between a resonator to a frame called a crossbar. The player plucks the strings with bare fingers. Orpheus's lyre may have looked something like this model. Its resonator was probably an empty tortoiseshell.

This magnificent lyre is called a bowl lyre. It comes from Ethiopia

The folk harp in the picture below comes from Peru. It has 28 strings. Each string is tuned to a particular note. If you run your finger across all the strings, you can play a pattern of notes which follow on from each other, called a scale. This is just like the scale you play when you run your finger over the white notes on a piano. Can you see the holes in the harp's resonator? These allow the resonating sound to escape.

A Peruvian harp player

In ancient times, lyres were popular all over the world. Today they are played mainly in parts of Africa, where they often accompany singing in religious festivals. The highly decorated lyre in the picture above comes from Ethiopia.

The lyre   The harp

Large and small harps

Harps are also made from strings attached to a frame. But harps are different from lyres in one important way. Look at the diagram above. You can see that the strings of the folk harp are set at an angle so that they run from the resonator to the instrument's neck. The lyre's strings run straight from the resonator to the crossbar. Harps are usually much larger than lyres.

Lutes with frets

If you were learning to play the violin, how would you know where to place your fingers to play the notes you want? Your teacher would need to show you where to press down on the fingerboard. Then, of course, you would have to practise and practise until you knew all the positions by heart and could play quickly and well.

On the fingerboard of some instruments, such as lutes and guitars, you will find ridges called frets. Frets are fixed across the fingerboard at certain intervals to help you to play the right note. When you press a string above a particular fret, the string vibrates only between the fret and the bridge on the resonator. Each fret marks a different note that a single string can play. When a string is pressed in this way, it is called 'stopping the string'. Frets mean you can learn where to place your fingers more easily.

1. Stopping a string without frets
2. Using frets to stop a string

1
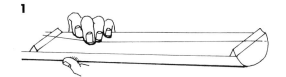

2
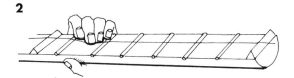

This picture, by the Italian artist Michelangelo Merisi da Caravaggio, is called *Young Man Playing a Lute*

A Chinese moon
guitar player

A Portuguese
fish lute

The lute family

Lutes are stringed instruments which are popular all over the world. They usually have frets to help the player produce a wide range of notes. The soft sound of a lute makes it the perfect instrument for accompanying songs.

Lutes come in many different shapes and sizes. The folk lute from China shown in the picture above is called a ch'in. It is also known as the moon guitar, because it has such a round body – just like a full moon. Many moon guitars are decorated in bright colours like this one.

The amazing Portuguese lute in the picture on the right has a body carved in the shape of a fish. This is the resonator. Can you see its sharp teeth and the detailed carved scales?

Strumming and plucking

A banjo

A ukulele

An American painting of a banjo player from the early 1800s

During the 1700s and 1800s, many thousands of Africans were brought to America to work as slaves. Many worked on the tobacco and cotton plantations in the southern states. In the picture at the bottom of the page you can see plantation workers dancing to the music of a banjo. The banjo is a stringed instrument which developed from long-necked lutes that were brought to America from Africa.

A banjo has between four and nine metal strings. Its body is round, with a skin or parchment stretched over it somewhat like a drum. A metal frame keeps the parchment firmly in place. The back of the banjo is often left open, so the noise it makes is not very resonant. Both banjos and ukuleles make a light, twangy sound when the strings are plucked with the fingertips.

Strum away

This large picture shows the British entertainer George Formby playing a ukulele. The ukulele comes from Hawaii and looks like a small guitar. You can see from the picture that it has four strings. Its name comes from a Hawaiian word meaning flea – because the ukulele is much smaller than a real guitar!

The strings are plucked with the fingers of one hand while the fingers of the other hand press the strings down on the fingerboard to make the different notes. Banjos and ukuleles can also be played in a different way by running the fingers over all the strings together. This makes a smoother sound and is known as strumming. You do not have to be able to read music to play instruments like the ukulele or the banjo. You just read a chart which tells you where to put your fingers.

Some people use a plectrum to pick the strings. This creates a different sound. They either hold the plectrum or fix it to their fingers, as you can see in the diagram below. You can read more about plectra on page 67.

The British ukulele player George Formby

Using a plectrum

The guitar

A Spanish guitar

Segovia

One of the most famous classical guitarists of all time was also a Spaniard. His name was Andrés Segovia. When Segovia was a boy, his parents did not approve of him playing the guitar. He had to practise in secret, without a teacher. He watched flamenco players and practised and studied, and practised some more. Eventually, all of Segovia's hard work paid off. His first concert, in Granada in 1909, was a great success and marked the beginning of Segovia's career as a brilliant guitarist.

A flamenco guitarist

When you think of the classical, or acoustic, guitar, you probably think of Spain and flamenco dancers stamping their feet to the exciting rhythm of a guitar. During the 1800s you would have heard a guitar being played in every village in Spain. It was the time when the guitar reached the peak of its popularity. Each of these guitars was based on a design by a Spanish instrument maker called Antonio Torres. In fact, all six-stringed, classical guitars, like the one in the picture above, are based upon Torres's original design. They have a wooden body which acts as a resonator, and a round soundhole to let out the musical sound.

The Spanish classical guitarist Andrés Segovia

A member of the Gypsy Kings folk group

Folk guitars

Guitars designed to play folk music are usually slightly different from the classical, Spanish guitar. Classical guitars usually have strings made of animal gut or nylon, while folk guitars usually have steel strings. Folk guitars also tend to have a narrower fingerboard. Folk players like the Gypsy Kings, a lively band from South America, hold the guitars high up across their bodies as they play fast Spanish rhythms.

The bottleneck

Folk musicians often need to hold down all the guitar strings as they strum. This can be difficult! To help them do this, they use a metal tube called a bottleneck, which you can see in the picture below.

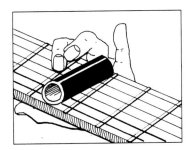

Using a bottleneck

The bottleneck is worn on a finger and touches several strings at once. The musician moves the bottleneck up and down the strings to produce an effective sliding sound.

Plectra

Many guitar players use a plectrum to pluck the strings. This protects their fingers as they play. Plectra come in different shapes and sizes. The most common kind has a pointed end to pluck the strings and a rounded end to hold. Some plectra are shaped to fit over the finger or thumb so that they can be worn rather than gripped. There are several different kinds of plectra in the picture below. As you can see, plectra can be made from metal or plastic.

Different kinds of plectra

Electric guitars

An electric guitar and amplifier

The electric guitar has the same name as the classical guitar, but it is a quite different instrument. You can see from the picture on the left that the electric guitar has a solid body. The vibrations of the strings are changed into electric signals. The signals are sent to a machine called an amplifier, which turn them back into sound. A loudspeaker then picks up the sound and increases it even further. The amplifier and loudspeaker are often housed in the same box, as they are in the picture. The result is a sound that is not at all like a Spanish guitar!

If you go to a music shop and look at the names of some of the electric guitars for sale, you will probably see a brand called Gibson. Orville Gibson was an American musician who developed the first electric guitars. Other kinds of electric guitars are also named after the people who developed them – Les Paul and Leo Fender are two other well-known names.

Special effects

A player can make an electric guitar
sound different by using one of the
special effects of an amplifier. If a
wobbly note is required, the player
presses a pedal known as a vibrator. A
fuzz-box produces a whirring sound. A
reverb makes an echo like the one you
get when you sing in the shower. The
wah-wah pedal does just what you would
expect – it makes the sound come and
go with a wailing wah-wah noise!

Playing the electric guitar

Playing the electric guitar is a skill which
depends very much on the player's own
personality. Most players are self-taught
and many prefer to be able to make up,
or improvise, the music they play instead
of playing something a composer has
already written down.

Rock and roll

In the 1950s, rock and roll exploded
onto the musical scene. Rock and roll
music is a mixture of folk, jazz and
rhythm and blues and the electric guitar
is an important instrument in this music.
The bass electric guitar was developed to
provide the low notes in a rock and roll
group. It usually has only four strings,
which are thicker and longer than the
strings on an ordinary guitar. Sometimes
bass guitars don't have frets.

Great players like the American guitarist
Jimi Hendrix showed the world that the
electric guitar could be made into as
personal an instrument as the human
voice. Look at Jimi Hendrix's expression
in this picture. He is completely involved
in his music!

The American
electric guitarist Jimi
Hendrix

An electric bass
guitar

Music on the page

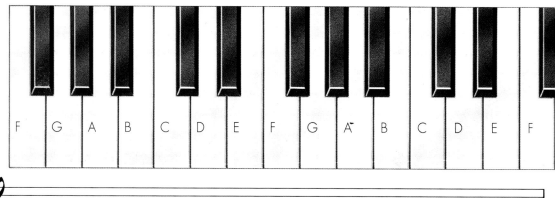

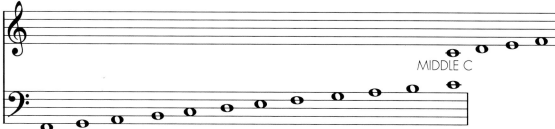

MIDDLE C

Composers write down their music. That way they can be sure that it will be performed just as they want it to be. Writing and reading music is like writing and reading words. But to write or read music you have to learn another language.

The language of music

Notes are like words – they make up the language of music. Musical notes are named after the first seven letters of the alphabet. The C nearest the middle of a keyboard is called middle C. Music is written on sets of five lines, each called staves. A stave is like a ladder. The higher up the ladder you are, the higher the note sounds.

At the beginning of each stave there is a sign called a clef. The treble clef 𝄞 shows that the notes are above middle C and the bass clef 𝄢 shows that the notes are below middle C.

The picture above shows you how the notes on a keyboard are written down on the staves. You can find out more about keyboards on pages 76–79.

Lengths of notes

Look at a metre rule. You'll see that it can be divided into 100 centimetres. And you know that a centimetre can be divided into 10 millimetres. Lengths of musical notes are measured in a similar way. Long notes can be divided up into shorter notes.

Let's start with a long note called a whole note (also called a semibreve). It is written like this 𝅝

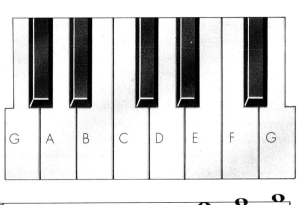

Every whole note is worth two half notes (or minims) 𝅗𝅥

Every half note is worth two quarter notes (or crotchets) 𝅘𝅥

Every quarter note is worth two eighth notes (or quavers) 𝅘𝅥𝅮

Music usually has regular groups of beats. When music is written down, it is written in sections called bars or measures.

Chords

When you want several notes to be played together, you write down all the notes and layer them one on top of the other. This layer is called a chord. A chord looks like this:

Scales

Music is usually based on a series of notes called a scale. You can use scales made up of different notes. Musical pieces from other parts of the world may sound strange to you because they are based on scales which are different from the one you are used to hearing.

Western music is usually based on a scale of eight notes. This scale goes from one note to the same note eight notes, or an octave, higher. For example, the scale of C goes C, D, E, F, G, A, B, C:

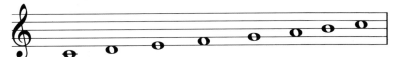

Chinese, Japanese, and most other eastern music is based on a 5-note scale called the pentatonic scale. It looks like this:

Eastern music is generally much freer and more individual than western music. People are encouraged to compose and improvise the music as they go along. Some Indian music uses notes that lie between the notes which are written in western music. Indian music is not usually written down. The musicians learn to play an instrument by ear, by copying and listening to great players. You can read more about this on the next page.

The sitar of India

You might also hear another background noise which is lower than the sympathetic strings. This is the sound of the drone strings, which make a continuous low tone below the main melody. When you listen to the sitar, you might think that there were two or three instruments playing together. Of course, this complicated arrangement of strings means that the sitar is a difficult instrument to play. Many new players learn from skilled sitar players.

This diagram shows you how the strings of a sitar are arranged

Ragas

Traditional Indian music is not written down. Performers learn groups of notes called ragas and develop their own way of playing them. They improvise the music as they go along. A raga is a combination of a scale and a melody. Each raga has its own mood, such as happiness, sorrow or peace. The different ragas are meant to be played at different times of the day or year. Musicians choose the raga very carefully, often not announcing until the last moment which one they intend to play.

An old Indian print of a sitar player

The sitar is the most popular instrument in northern India. If you look at the picture of the sitar you will see that it has a complicated arrangement of strings. Six or seven main strings are played with a wire plectrum. The strings run over frets, which are like metal hoops. You can move the frets to different positions. Under the main strings there are between 9 and 13 other strings, called sympathetic strings. These strings vibrate when the main strings are played.

A sitar

A special sound

The Indian musician Ravi Shankar is one of the best-known sitar players in the world. Look at the picture below. Can you see how hard Ravi Shankar concentrates as he plays? His music swoops and slides to the accompaniment of special drums called tablas. Audiences all over the world have been amazed by his playing.

Ravi Shankar has performed to enthusiastic listeners in western countries. The violinist Yehudi Menuhin and the pop group The Beatles have both performed with him, making an interesting mix of the music of east and west.

The Indian sitar player Ravi Shankar

The world of zithers

Many instruments are made up of part of one instrument and part of another. The zither is an instrument which is partly a harp and partly a lute. It has several strings which stretch from one end of the instrument to the other. Some zithers are plucked like harps, while others are stopped with the fingers and plucked, like the strings of a lute.

The simplest zithers are made from a hollowed-out piece of wood. A length of string is laced backwards and forwards across the zither and supported by wooden sticks as bridges at either end. This kind of zither is called a tube zither.

Many tube zithers have a slit cut into the top which acts as a soundhole. This means that the twanging strings sound more resonant. Tube zithers are most common in Africa, where they are played as accompanying instruments.

Make your own tube zither

You could make a simple tube zither from an old plastic bottle. Ask an adult to help you cut a wide slit lengthwise along one side of the bottle. Tie some string tightly around each end of the cylinder. Cut some pieces of string and thread a bead onto each one. Now tie the strings onto the string at each end of the bottle. Paint the bottle in bright colours or decorate it with cut-out pictures to give it a more authentic look.

Now try playing your zither. You may need to tighten your strings to get an effective sound. You can also use stretched rubber bands as your strings. How does this change the sound?

Long zithers

In China and Japan, you often see zithers which are so long that they need to be rested on the floor or on a low table to be played. The koto, from Korea, has 13 strings made of silk. The strings rest on high bridges which are movable. The player alters the pitch of

the note by moving the bridges backwards and forwards. In the picture you can see the player's right hand plucking the strings and the left hand pressing the strings against the bridges to create notes of different pitch.

The dulcimer

The dulcimer is a kind of zither which is often used to play folk music in the countries of eastern Europe but they are found all over the world. The strings can be plucked or, more usually, hit with small wooden hammers. Sometimes the heads of these hammers are double-sided, with one side made of soft leather and the other of hard leather. This means that soft and loud sounds can be produced. The strings vibrate for a long

time after they are hit, so the sounds become blurred. Can you see a dulcimer being played in the Tibetan village orchestra in the picture below?

A South Korean koto player

A Tibetan village orchestra

Playing the keys

A keyboard

Did you know that a keyboard instrument like the piano is actually a stringed instrument? If you open the lid of a piano and look inside, you will see the strings. There are three kinds of stringed keyboard instruments. They are the clavichord, the harpsichord and the piano. All three use a different way of sounding the strings. The oldest of the group is the clavichord, which dates back to about 1400. The clavichord makes a very soft musical sound.

Playing a clavichord

Inside a clavichord

This diagram shows how the clavichord strings are played. When you press down one of the keys on the keyboard, a piece of metal called a tangent shoots up and hits a pair of strings. This makes the strings vibrate. The tangent stays in contact with the strings until you take your finger off the key. It drops back into position and the note finishes when the string stops vibrating.

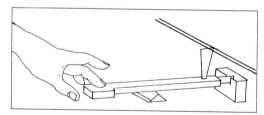

A tangent hits a clavichord string to make it vibrate

The clavichord is a small instrument. Some clavichords do not have legs and are rested on a table to be played. The quietness of clavichord music means that it is better suited to personal performances in a small room than to a performance in a large concert hall. Clavichords are being made again today and are popular among people who like to play old music on the right kind of instrument.

The harpsichord

The picture on the right is a harpsichord. You can see that it looks like a grand piano, although it doesn't sound like one. It has a bright, twangy tone. Look at the diagram below to see how a harpsichord's strings are sounded. They are plucked, not hit. When you press down on a harpsichord key, a plectrum made of a strip of plastic or leather jumps up and plucks the string, making it sound. The note dies away as soon as the key is released. The harpsichord makes a clear, crisp musical sound, which can be very powerful.

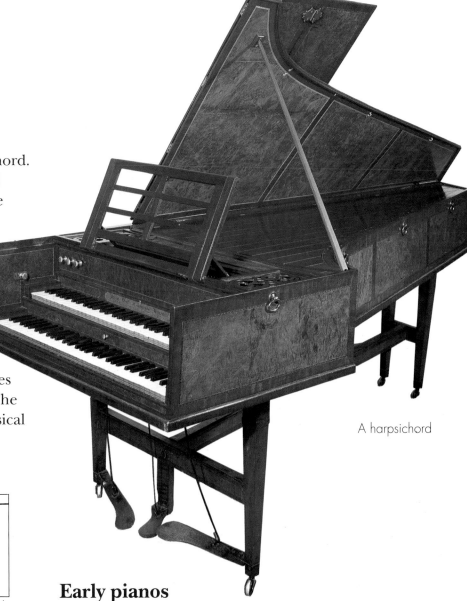

A harpsichord

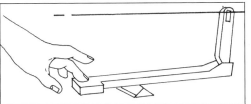

A plectrum plucks
a harpsichord string
to make it sound

Some harpsichords have two keyboards, or manuals. They also have pedals and controls, called stops, which help the player to create different sounds – loud or soft. The harpsichord was a very popular instrument between about 1600 and 1800. Today, it is used mainly to perform music written during that period by composers such as the famous German composer Johann Sebastian Bach.

Early pianos

The first piano was made in the early 1700s by the Italian Bartolomeo Cristofori. He designed his instrument so that the strings were struck by a padded hammer which immediately fell away from the string. This happened whether or not the player had released the key. As a result, the player could directly affect the sound the instrument made by the way he or she touched the keys. A gentle touch made a gentle noise, a drumming touch made a striking noise and smooth playing helped to join the notes together.

The versatile piano

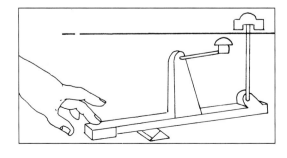

A caricature of the Hungarian composer and pianist Franz Liszt

The musician crouches over his piano keyboard, his long hair flops over his face, while his fingers thunder over the keys at an incredible speed. The caricature above shows the Hungarian pianist Franz Liszt who lived in the 1800s. His performances amazed his audiences because he played incredibly difficult sequences and hardly ever made a mistake. But Liszt was not only a brilliant pianist, he was also a composer.

Strengthening the instrument

In the time of Liszt, pianos were not as strongly built as they are today. So after only a short burst of Liszt's ferocious playing, the piano sometimes fell to pieces!

Piano makers have improved the instrument a great deal over the years. A modern piano has an iron frame with steel strings stretched over it. The strings are stretched at very high tension, so the frame needs to be very strong. High notes have three strings each, middle notes two and low bass notes have just one thick string. Behind the strings is a soundboard, which resonates when the strings vibrate.

The inside story

The diagram below shows you what happens inside the piano when you press down on a key on the keyboard. First, a hammer strikes the strings, making it vibrate. If it went on vibrating after you went on to play other notes, the sound would become blurred. To prevent this, each note has a damper. A damper is a small pad which falls sharply against the strings when you let go of the key and stops the string from vibrating.

A hammer strikes the piano string to make it vibrate

Music for pianos

The piano provides a wide range of notes and many composers have written wonderful music for it. Composers of the 1700s, such as the Austrian Wolfgang Amadeus Mozart, wrote splendid music for the piano. But pianos in Mozart's time had a quieter, drier tone than we are now used to hearing and many people think that Mozart's music sounds best when it is played on an old instrument. Have you ever played the piano? If you have, you probably know that pianos come in different sizes.

A grand piano

The grand piano

You can play on an upright piano which fits into a small room, or you might be lucky enough to play on a concert grand piano, like the one in the picture. It is 3 metres long and takes up a lot more space. You really need a concert hall to play a grand piano in! However, whatever size you play, the piano has to be the greatest of all solo instruments!

Playing together in an orchestra

Have you ever been to a concert where the music is played by an orchestra? If so, you'll have sat eagerly waiting while the players came onto the stage, carrying their instruments. The violinists tighten their bows and make sure their chin rests are comfortable. The cellists adjust their spikes. The oboe player plays an A note. All the other players tune their instruments to match the oboe's A. Finally, when all is ready, the conductor comes on stage and raises the white stick, or baton. There is silence.

The baton comes down and the orchestra starts to play. The concert has begun!

The conductor's job

A large orchestra can have as many as 100 musicians playing together. No wonder it makes an impressive noise! To keep the performance under control, the orchestra needs a conductor. The conductor keeps the players in time and guides the mood of the music.

The BBC Symphony Orchestra, London

He uses movements of his baton and facial expressions to tell the musicians when to play quietly, when to play loudly, when to start and stop or when to slow down or draw the music out. Try conducting some taped music using a small stick or ruler as a baton.

Behind the scenes

When you see an orchestra playing, you may think the conductor's job is an easy one. It may look as if all that is required is to stand there and beat time! But behind all this are long hours of practice time, called rehearsals, which the conductor has put in with the players. The conductor tells the orchestra how the music is to be interpreted. What do you think would happen if the conductor left the orchestra to play by itself? The sound could soon become disorganized.

Every conductor has a strong idea about how a piece of music should sound. If you can, try to compare two recordings of the same music with different conductors. You might hear some interesting differences!

1. play quietly
2. play loudly
3. come in
4. play expressively
5. stop playing

This drawng shows where the musicians in an orchestra sit

The human voice

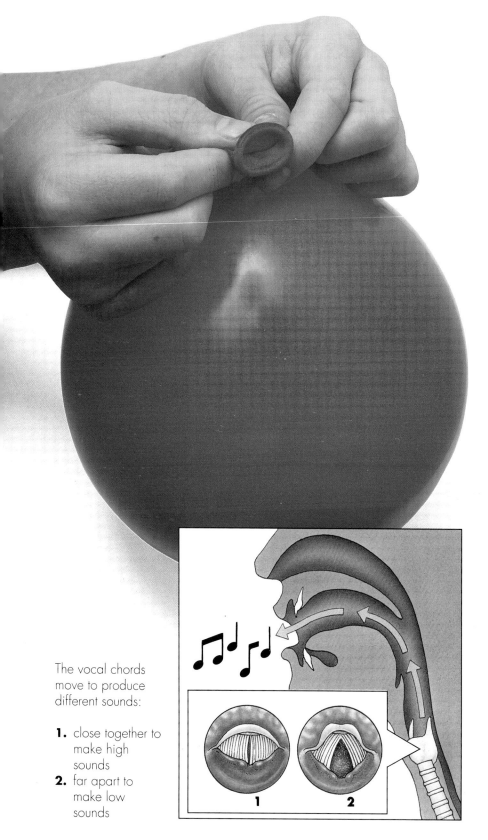

The vocal chords move to produce different sounds:

1. close together to make high sounds
2. far apart to make low sounds

Take a deep breath. Now sing any note you like, letting the air out slowly. Can you feel your throat vibrating as the air comes out? It may seem unlikely, but your voice is a stringed instrument. It has its own vibrating strings and resonator in just the same way as a stringed instrument like a guitar does.

Your strings are the vocal cords in your voicebox, or larynx. Vocal cords are ribbons of skin which stretch across the larynx – you can see them in the picture below. When you sing or talk, air is forced across the cords, making them vibrate. You can see for yourself how your larynx works. If you blow up a balloon and stretch the neck to make a narrow slit, you'll hear a screeching noise as the air rushes out. That's just what happens in your larynx, only your voice sounds better than the balloon!

Now try humming through your nose. Can you feel your nose buzzing? That's because your nose is one of your voice's resonators. The vibrations also resonate in your head, mouth, throat and chest.

High and low

You sing high notes by tightening your vocal cords. As you come down the scale, the cords become looser. Everyone has his or her own comfortable range. The highest singing voice is the soprano. In a child, this is known as treble. Then comes the alto (called counter tenor in a man). Men usually sing in one of two ranges – either tenor or bass.

The famous Italian opera singer Luciano Pavarotti

Ways of using your voice

There are many different styles of singing. You can probably think of several. You may have heard a folk singer crooning softly or the clear tones of a choirboy. Maybe you have heard an Islamic preacher, or muezzin, calling people to prayer in a mosque or an Austrian's yodelling call echoing back from a mountainside. Pop and rock singers use microphones to make their voices sound louder, so they can sing quite softly and still be heard by a large audience. You can use your personal stringed instrument to sing whenever you feel like it!

A microphone

Singing in groups

A choir

The music of a group of singers, called a choir, was an important part of church services in medieval Europe. Monks in monasteries used to sing all of the services in Latin. Today, you might hear music sung by choirs which is based on this church tradition. It is called choral music.

Singing a story

Many people enjoy taking part in large-scale musical performances called oratorios. Oratorios are based on Bible stories from the Jewish and Christian religions, but they do not have to be performed in church.

Orations are performed by an orchestra, a choir and soloists, who sing important parts on their own. A special singer called a narrator tells the story in song. The German composer Johann Sebastian Bach is well known for his church cantatas. A cantata is a story sung by one or two singers who are accompanied by various instruments.

The German composer Johann Sebastian Bach

Gospel music

Gospel music is a kind of church singing which combines elements of hymns, jazz and black American religious folksongs. Gospel choirs like the one in the picture below sing with great warmth and emotion. A gospel concert always involves the audience, who end up stamping, clapping their hands and dancing. It's great fun!

Other groups

Not all singing groups are choirs, of course. You can probably think of many other kinds of singing musical groups. There are pop and rock bands, folk singers, jazz bands and many more. All these groups use the distinctive sound of voices singing together.

Popular music

Most pop groups use their voices as well as their instruments to make music. You probably know all the words of many pop songs which are popular today. You'll know that some of these pop groups are only popular for a short time. A new group takes their place and they are soon forgotten.

But there are exceptions. The British group called The Beatles wrote and performed songs in the 1960s and 1970s that seem likely to remain popular for a long time to come. Perhaps you have a favourite pop group at the moment. Do you think their songs will still be popular in 350 years' time? That's how long ago Bach wrote his choral music!

An American
gospel choir

Listening to opera

The opera singer
Kiri Te Kanawa

What IS she singing about? She is making a lovely sound, but you can't understand the words! These thoughts might cross your mind if you were listening to a musical play called an opera. The German composer Richard Wagner wrote what he called music-dramas. He wrote both words and music. Built into the music were themes that represented characters or ideas in the story. So unless you do your homework on a Wagner opera and you speak German, you might find it difficult to understand what is happening.

Early opera

Opera began in Italy around 1600. It began when composers put music to a story. This kind of singing is called recitative. The Italian composer Claudio Monteverdi made the opera style livelier by adding choruses and dances, although he kept to the recitative for telling the story.

During the 1600s, opera became very popular and composers wrote more and more of them to satisfy public demand. The stories were often quite fantastic

A scene from the opera *Turandot*

and the operas were often specially designed to show off the voice of a famous singer. But in the 1700s, the Austrian composer Wolfgang Amadeus Mozart wrote both serious operas that were entertaining and comic operas that were well written. The standard of opera rose to new heights.

Grand opera

The grand opera of the 1800s is what many people today think of as true opera. It has colourful costumes, romantic music and extravagant acting. These operas are still popular today, with lavish performances like this scene from *Turandot*, an opera by the Italian composer Giacomo Puccini. The great modern opera singers, like the New Zealand opera star Kiri Te Kanawa, draw huge audiences to each performance.

So, even if you do have difficulty following the words of an opera, you can still enjoy the drama of the performance. Or perhaps you would prefer to see a musical? This is a modern

form of opera, somewhere between classical or grand opera and an evening of popular music, which also offers dancing and catchy tunes.

A programme from a modern musical

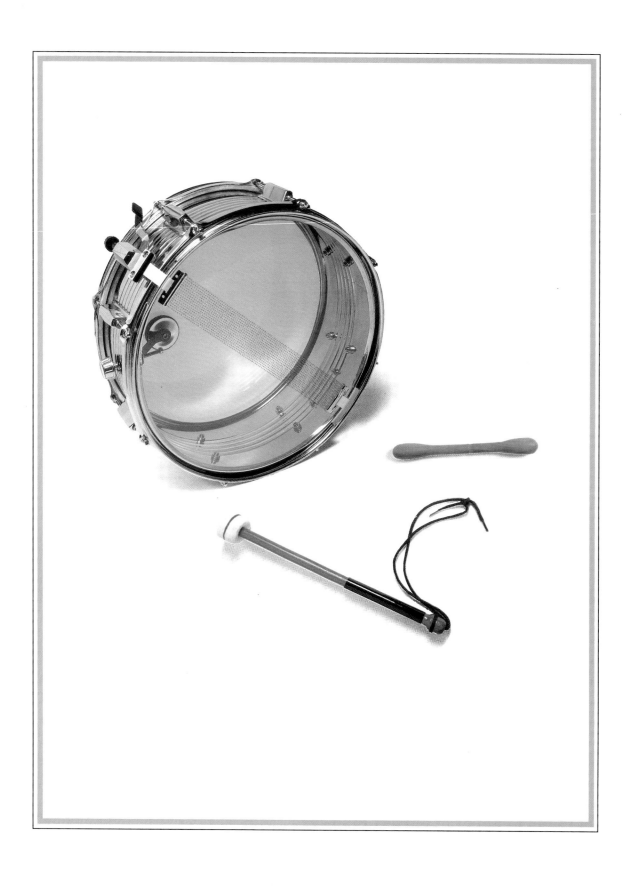

— CHAPTER THREE —

BEATING THE DRUM

Beating a drum is an extremely ancient form of music-making. To many people, drums are still an important part of rituals and ceremonies, and are often used to set the mood of an occasion.

You will see in this chapter that some drums are played on their own. Sometimes one musician plays several drums at once. And sometimes drums are played with other instruments, providing a steady beat that keeps the music moving on.

You will find out how you can make your own drum and decorate it in any way you choose. And you will find suggestions on how to make all sorts of different sounds from the same drum.

What is percussion?

A drummer playing
at a wedding in
southern India

Listen to the noises around you. Can you hear a ticking clock, a radio playing or the hum of a car engine? Thousands of years ago, people listened to the sounds around them, too. They heard the roar of animals, the crash of thunder, the rush of a river. And people started to imitate the sounds around them with sounds of their own. They clapped their hands and stamped their feet or used sticks and stones to make distinct noises.

This was how instruments that you hit, shake, or scrape came to be. We call them percussion instruments. Gradually, these early instruments became more complicated. Banging a piece of wood made one sound. If the wood was hollowed out, the sound improved. And if a piece of animal skin was stretched over the hollowed wood, the sound was even better. Drums like this dating from prehistoric times have been discovered.

Noise from vibrations

A drum is a very simple instrument. It can be made by tightly stretching a thin skin, or membrane, over a simple frame. The beat sound arises when you tap on the skin with your fingers or hands, like the drummer in the picture. Or you can use a beater. The drummer in the second picture is using two sticks to beat his drums. This makes the skin shake, or vibrate, with tiny movements, and as the skin vibrates, so does the air around it. We call these air vibrations sound waves.

When the sound waves spread down into the hollow part of the drum, they echo around and grow louder. When sound waves act like this, we call it resonating.

Make a drum

You can easily make your own drum. Find a mixing bowl or a tin. Stretch waxed paper or cloth tightly over the top. Fasten it over the rim with string or a rubber band. Or you can use lengths of overlapping tape to make the membrane. Tap the top of the drum gently with a pencil or a spoon. If you scatter a few grains of salt on the membrane, you'll be able to see how the vibration causes the salt to bounce.

Can you hear the note the drum makes? Press lightly on one edge of the paper and tap it again. Is the note higher this time? It should be! That's because you have made the membrane tighter. The tightness of a membrane is known as its tension.

A drummer from Ghana

How do you hear sounds?

Did you realize you have two drums inside your head? They are your eardrums! Each eardrum is a membrane that works in much the same way as the drum that you hit. Your outer ear acts like a funnel collecting sound waves from the air around you. The sound travels down a tube called the ear canal until it hits your eardrum. The sound waves make the eardrum vibrate. The vibrations travel inward to some tiny bones in the inner ear.

Now the vibrations are twenty times stronger. They are passed to the cochlea, which contains three tubes coiled like a snail's shell. The tubes are full of liquid.

When vibrations reach the cochlea, they make the liquid move. This moves hairs in one of the coils, which in turn causes nerve endings to send messages to the brain. These tell you all about the sound you've heard. The way we hear sounds is a complicated process – and we are not even aware that it's happening.

How loud is loud?

The loudness of a sound is measured on a scale of units called decibels. Very loud sounds, such as explosions, have the highest decibel reading. They can burst your eardrum, so people who work with noisy machinery wear ear protectors.

A diagram of the ear, showing:

1. outer ear
2. ear canal
3. eardrum
4. bones
5. cochlea

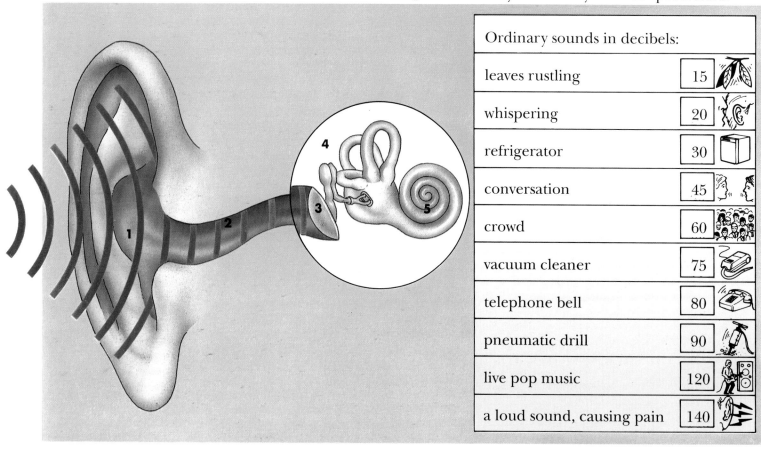

Ordinary sounds in decibels:	
leaves rustling	15
whispering	20
refrigerator	30
conversation	45
crowd	60
vacuum cleaner	75
telephone bell	80
pneumatic drill	90
live pop music	120
a loud sound, causing pain	140

The German composer Ludwig van Beethoven

Hearing difficulties

In the past, people with poor hearing used a large funnel called an ear trumpet to help them hear better. When they held it to their ear, the trumpet shape acted like a large second ear, collecting more sound. The great German composer Ludwig van Beethoven used an ear trumpet when he was becoming deaf. Today, technology provides electronic hearing aids, which are much more efficient than ear trumpets. And even people who can't hear can play musical instruments. This picture shows the Scottish percussionist Evelyn Glennie. Despite being deaf, she is one of the most skillful percussionists in the world today.

The Scottish percussionist Evelyn Glennie

Different kinds of drums

Drums are made all over the world, and traditionally they have been made from whatever materials were on hand. Drums are often made of wood, but can also be made of clay or metal. In Arctic regions there are no trees, so the Eskimo people, the Inuits, might use bone as a frame for a drum. The membrane is usually made of animal skin. Of course, the type of skin also depends on what is available. Drum membranes have been made from snakeskin and even from elephants' ears.

Adding paste

Some Indian and African drum makers rub a circular patch of paste onto the membrane of their drum. In Africa, the paste is usually made from a mixture of beeswax and roasted peanut powder. In India they use rice and ashes. When the player beats on the special patch, the sound produced is lower than in other places on the membrane.

Pastes made from rice, peanut powder, beeswax and ashes

1

Thin and fat

Drums come in many different shapes and sizes. The pictures above show you the six main shapes. The barrel drum has a membrane at each end, so it is played on its side. Some barrel drums have only one membrane and can be stood on end to be played. Waisted drums have a pinched-in waist. They can also have one or two membranes. Goblet drums are shaped like drinking cups or glasses. They have a wide membrane at the top and a narrow foot to support them on the ground.

Long drums are tall and thin, with a single membrane. Frame drums have one membrane stretched over a shallow frame, which is usually round. Finally, there are vessel drums which are bowl-shaped drums with a single membrane. These are also called kettledrums because kettle is an old word for a cooking pot.

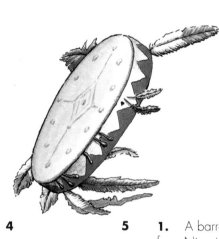
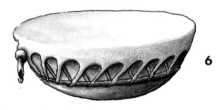

2 **3** **4** **5**

1. A barrel drum from Nigeria
2. A waisted drum from Japan
3. A goblet drum from Ghana
4. A long drum from New Guinea
5. A North American Indian frame drum
6. A kettledrum from India

Making a noise

Drums are often used to accompany dancing, as in this picture showing Chinese dancers. They are also used in religious ceremonies, for sending messages, for frightening an enemy or as a way of praying for good weather. In Europe in the 1500s, they were even used by dentists. While a patient was having a tooth pulled out, a drum was beaten to drown out the yells!

6

Dancing drummers from China

Sounding a drum

This drummer is part of an Indian picture called *Three Musicians and a Dancing Girl*

Wire brushes and felt-headed beaters

To make a drum sound, you have to make the drum's membrane vibrate by hitting it. You already know that you can strike a drum with your fingers or hands or use drum sticks or beaters. Small drums such as the Indian one in this picture are usually played with the fingers or hands. The larger drums, such as the bass drum, are usually played with beaters. Look at the sticks and beaters in the picture below. You will see that some have padded ends. Can you see the wire brush? This makes a swishing sound when it hits the membrane.

The type of drum-hitter you use makes all the difference to the sound your drum makes. If you hit a drum with a stick, it makes a hard, clear sound. If you hit it with a padded beater, it sounds softer and muffled. Try hitting a homemade drum with any stick-shaped thing you can find – a wooden spoon, a hairbrush or a bunch of twigs. They will all produce interesting noises from your drum.

Beater heads

The padding on the heads of beaters can be made from felt, leather, wood, cork, rubber or plastic. You could use other materials to make your own beaters.

You will need some thin sticks, about 20 centimetres long, and anything you can think of to make a soft head. Look at this picture for some ideas. To make a soft beater, cut a round piece of cloth and fill it with cotton wool. Wrap it round the stick and tie it on. For a harder beater, you could trim the sides of a large cork to make it round, or you could try fixing a small rubber ball to the end of a stick. Or you could wrap lots of rubber bands around the stick until you have a rounded shape.

Now you can experiment with the different beaters. But be careful when you beat your homemade drum. If you hit the membrane too hard, you might make a hole in it.

Beaters made at home

Rhythm and pulse

You know that drums produce a strong, repetitive pattern of sound called a rhythm. If you march along like the girl above, your feet make a rhythm. You can write this marching rhythm down as music. You have to use a mark to represent each distinct footstep. These marks are called notes and when the notes making up your rhythm are written, they look like this:

You'll see there are two notes in every section, or bar. We call these notes pulses, or beats. The pulse is the heartbeat of music. A doctor has to feel your pulse to find out how regularly your heart is beating, but you can hear the beat in music just by listening!

Most western music is made up of regular patterns of beats. It is these patterns of beats which make up the rhythm of a piece of music. Modern composers arrange groups of beats in many different ways to make interesting rhythms. If you listen to a piece of music called *The Rite of Spring*, by the Russian composer Igor Stravinsky, you will hear some very unusual and exciting rhythms.

A group of drummers from Rwanda beat out a rhythm

Marching beat

Accents and rest

Most western music has a rhythm of two or three beats. But how can we tell when the beats fall, when each one is followed by thousands of other notes which make up the piece of music? The answer is that certain notes in the group are more strongly stressed than others. They are accented.

The next time you listen to some music, see if you can tell where the accented notes are. Listen to marches that follow a **one**-two, **one**-two beat, or rock songs which stress the first of four beats – **one**, two, three, four. If you listen carefully, you will be able to count how many beats there are in each bar.

Composers sometimes change the normal pulse by putting accents on beats that you would expect to be unaccented. This is called syncopation. You will often hear syncopated rhythms in jazz. Sometimes there's a gap, or rest, in the music, when the instrument does not play. These rests also make up part of the rhythmical pattern.

African rhythms

You can hear some exciting rhythms in African music. In some musical groups, there may be as many as twelve musicians, all playing different rhythms at the same time. Each player follows a set pattern of rhythm which fits into the patterns played by the rest of the drummers.

Rhythms in eastern music

Much of the music of India and other parts of Asia does not follow the same regular rhythm patterns as western music. Eastern music is often not written down. Instead, it is made up by the musicians as they play, using complicated rules of rhythm. You can read more about drumming in India on pages 108 and 109.

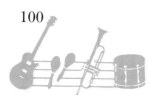

Talking drums

A talking drummer from Nigeria

In some languages of the world, the same word can be spoken in two ways to give two quite different meanings. If you say the word in a high tone, it means something completely different from the same word spoken in a low tone.

One such language is Yoruba, spoken by the people of northern Nigeria. These people use drums to send messages in Yoruba. They use a large drum for the low tones and a small one for the high tones. In this way, a drummer can send messages to people up to 30 kilometres away. Some Nigerian drummers are so skillful that they can send messages using only one drum, like the one in the picture. But how do they vary the tones so that their drums 'talk'?

You can change the tone of a drum by changing the tension of the membrane. A tighter membrane gives a higher tone. The membrane can be firmly attached to the body of the drum by gluing, nailing or lacing. Lacing is done in different patterns, as you can see in the pictures below.

Different patterns of lacing:

1. N lacing
2. W lacing
3. X lacing
4. Y lacing
5. Net lacing

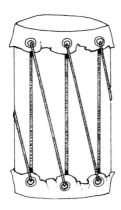

1

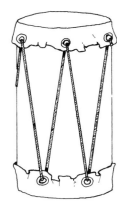

2

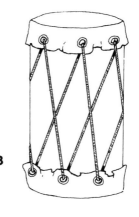

3

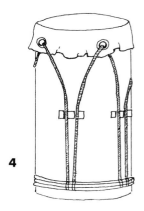

4

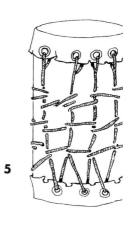

5

A Nigerian talking drum

Tapping out words

You can use a beater and your homemade drum to tap out the rhythm of people's names. Even when two words have the same number of syllables, their rhythmic patterns can be quite different. Try tapping 'tambourine' and then 'Africa'. You will hear that the rhythms are different. Some speech rhythms are fun to copy. Or try your favourite rhyme. But beware! English is not a tone language, like Yoruba, so 'shut the door' will sound the same as 'spill the beans'.

N-shaped lacing

The talking drum of Nigeria is laced very simply. The picture above shows you the tight N-shaped lacing in detail. As the drummer strikes the drum, using a crooked L-shaped beater, he adjusts the tightness of the lacing with the other hand. He pulls the membrane tighter to give a higher tone, or relaxes it to make the tone lower.

A drum on a frame

The Irish folk group
The Chieftains

Old Irish tales say that there was once only one drum in all of Ireland. It was shared by two friends. One day, they both needed the drum at the same time and could not agree on who should have it. They asked the advice of a wise man, who told them to cut the drum in two. The friends each went away with half the drum. And that, so the story says, is why the Irish drum, called the bodhran, has only one skin! The bodhran, pronounced 'bawren', is the favourite drum in Irish folk music. You can see one being played by a member of the Irish folk band The Chieftains in the picture.

Gentle or exciting

The bodhran can accompany a sad love song, beat a rousing march and urge on the energetic Irish dance called the reel. The sound of a bodhran depends on how it's made. The membrane was traditionally made of goatskin and the frame of ash wood.

A pin

A flick of the wrist

Playing the bodhran requires great skill. You hold the sticks at the back of the drum with your left hand. In your right hand, you hold the double-headed drumstick, called a pin. Look at the picture above to see what a pin looks like. You hold it like a pencil and flick your wrist backwards and forwards hitting the skin with both ends of the pin.

A drummer from Siberia

Magical powers

Another type of drum is played by people in northern Russia and by North American Indians. It is usually round, like the Siberian drum in the picture. An animal skin is stretched over the frame and the player holds the lacing like a handle. This kind of drum was mainly used to accompany sacred songs and rituals. It was also used to help communicate with the spirits of dead people or to pray for good weather. It was even thought to have magical powers in the hands of a medicine man.

Friction drums

An engraving of a rommelpot player by the Dutch artist Frans Hals

Friction is another way of saying rubbing. If you lick your finger and rub it over a tight drum membrane, it makes a grinding noise. Most friction drums have a hole in the drum membrane and a stick pushed into the hole makes a dramatic growling sound when it is rubbed round and round or up and down. The stick makes the whole drum vibrate.

Rommelpots

Rommelpots were popular friction drums in Europe. This picture of a rommelpot player is by the Dutch artist Frans Hals. Children used to make them out of a kitchen pot which they covered with an animal skin. They sometimes used mustard jars or even thimbles. Then they pierced the skin with a wet stick and rubbed the stick up and down. These rommelpots were often played at celebrations and religious festivals.

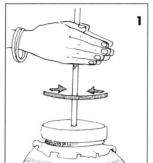

1. Rubbing the stick between the hands to turn it
2. Pulling the stick up and down

The lion roar

Friction drums like the one in the picture below are sometimes used in bands and orchestras. These drums have a string passed through the drumhead instead of a stick. The string is rubbed with the same soft sticky gum called resin that is used for violin bows. When you slide a piece of soft leather up the string, you get a gravelly, growling noise. This noise gives the drum its name.

Moving the stick

The beautiful friction drum in the picture above is from Zambia. You can see the stick piercing its membrane. The diagrams at the top of the page show you how the stick is moved to make a sound. It can be pulled up and down or turned by rubbing it between the hands.

An English lion roar drum

Mirlitons and pellet drums

If you wrap a piece of tissue paper round a comb, put your lips on the paper and hum or sing, your voice will be disguised. It will make a strange buzzing sound! This happens because the air coming out of your mouth makes the tissue paper membrane vibrate. You feel the vibrations tickling your lips as you blow.

Your tissue paper and comb are creating a mirliton. A mirliton is not so much a musical instrument as a gadget for changing the sound of a musical note.

Mirlitons can also be made from a cow's horn or from a dried hollow vegetable called a gourd. A thin membrane made from the web-like material which spiders spin to protect their eggs, or from parts of a bat's wing, provides the buzzing sound.

Two or three hundred years ago, European eunuch flutes worked in the same way. These instruments were also known as onion flutes, because onion skins were sometimes used as membranes. The player spoke or sang into the membrane over the hole at the end of the instrument.

A French eunuch flute

A modern kazoo

A kazoo is a toy mirliton with a tissue paper membrane located half-way down its length. You can see the circle of paper at the side of the picture. When you sing or talk into the tube, the paper vibrates to make your voice sound different, just like the tissue paper around your comb.

A pellet drum
from Tibet

Pellet drum

Drums like the Tibetan drum in the picture above are unusual because they are not played with hands or sticks. They are played with beads or pellets. Two frames are joined together, with each open end covered with a membrane. A string with pellets attached is tied around the middle.

When the drum is shaken, the pellets hit against the membrane, first at one end and then at the other. The Tibetan drum is gruesome as well as unusual. It is made from two human skulls which have been cut in half! Each half is covered by a membrane. These are hit by the bead on the string.

Make a yoghurt pot drum

Cover the open ends of two yoghurt pots with some waxed paper and attach it tightly with string or rubber bands.

Then glue the pots together, with the paper-covered ends facing outwards. Thread some beads onto string, making sure that the string is the right length to hit the paper at each end of the drum. Tie the string around the middle and your drum is ready to play.

Indian drums

Pairs of drums

The tabla are the drums you see being used most often by small groups of musicians in India. Tabla is the name for a pair of drums. The larger drum, called the bhaya, has a metal body. The smaller one, the tabla, has a wooden body. The tabla is always positioned on the drummer's right-hand side and the bhaya on the left.

The tabla

Playing the tabla

Indian drummers are said to be the best in the world. They can hear the difference between 15 and 16 very fast beats in a bar. Ask a friend to beat on the table 15 times and then again 16 times. Can you hear the difference? A drummer needs years and years of learning and practice to become so skilled in hearing rhythm.

A tabla from southern India

One hand or two

The drummer must learn to play each drum on its own and both drums at the same time. And the tabla can be played with one hand or with both hands together! Drummers usually squat on the ground and cradle the drums in their lap to play them. Each drum has a different tone, one higher than the other.

The sound each drum makes can be changed by spreading paste over the membrane. Small blocks of wood can also be placed under the lacing of the tabla to tighten the membrane and make the tone higher.

Finding the rhythm

Tabla players often play in a group, with musicians playing two stringed instruments called the sitar and the tambura. The music is not written down but is made up as the players go along. The drums play in a rhythm called a tala. A tala is a regular beat which the player uses throughout the piece of music. There can be anything from 3 to 100 beats in every bar and rhythms of 5, 5, 11 or 14 beats in a bar are quite usual. A special rhythm, called the Savari rhythm, has 11 beats in a bar, divided into sections of 4, 4, 1½ and 1½ beats. If you turn back to pages 98 and 99 to see that most western music has two or three beats in a bar, you will see how complicated the tala rhythm is.

The bhaya

Music in the world of Islam

It seems quite natural for us to have music whenever we want it. We can sing, we can play an instrument, we can listen to a tape. But it has not always been like this everywhere in the world. The prophet Mohammed, who founded the Islamic religion, did not approve of musical instruments. In the early days, singing was allowed, but only for religious purposes. A singer could chant from The Koran and call people to the mosque to pray.

As time went by, people performed more kinds of music and introduced more kinds of instruments. This is why Islamic music may have started as a single tune without any extra notes. People made up the music as they sang or drummed.

Using drums

Arab people played many different musical instruments. You can see a band of Arabic musicians playing lively music on various instruments at the top of the page. Drums were especially popular. They were used in marriage celebrations and great religious festivals. Military processions were accompanied by drumming.

The darbuka

So what were Arabic drums like? Frame drums, like the one in the top picture, were popular, and kettledrums were used for military processions. But the most beautiful drum to look at was a goblet drum called the darbuka.

A pair of darbukas

A painted darbuka from the Middle East

The darbuka is a goblet-shaped drum made from pottery or wood. You can see that the darbuka was beautifully painted and some were decorated with mosaic patterns of gleaming tortoiseshell and mother-of-pearl.

Darbuka are small drums, so they are easy to carry. Players in Iraq tuck them under their arm and hit them from the side with flat hands. The player can stand up or sit down like the drummer in the picture on the right. Sometimes the hitting surface is raised above the rim of the drum to make it easier to play.

Playing the darbuka

Drums for dancing

Music and dance played an important part in the lives of North American Apache Indians. Look at the picture below. The Apaches are dancing at a celebration. They circle the campfire, linking arms in a line as a singer sings in a high nasal voice. The dancers move four steps forwards and then back again. Gradually, the whole circle moves clockwise round the fire in a steady rhythm. The water drum played by the crouching drummer in the foreground provides this rhythm.

Loosened by water

American Indian water drums were made from an iron kettle, with a membrane of tanned buckskin. The drum was one-third full of water. As the drum was played, water splashed against the skin. This loosened the skin to make an interesting sound. The drummer beat the skin with a thin drumstick which had a loop at the end. The soft booming noise was quite unlike the sound of any other type of drum.

An Apache social dance

Samba dancers at the carnival in Rio de Janeiro, Brazil

Latin American rhythms

Ask anyone what makes Latin American music different from other music and you'll probably get one answer – rhythm. Drummers beat out the rhythms with such energy and enthusiasm that it's impossible not to get up and dance. Have you heard of the rumba, or the samba, or the bossa nova? These are all Latin American dances with special rhythms. Perhaps you can do one of them!

Latin American dance bands usually have more than one drum. The smallest ones are the bongos. Bongos are a pair of small drums which are open at the bottom. One drum is a little bigger than the other, so they play different notes. The drums are held between the knees and played with the fingers and hands, making a high, dry, tapping noise.

Timbales are similar to the bongos, but larger. Barrel-shaped congas are the largest drums in the band.

There are usually two or three congas in each dance band. They can be played with a cupped hand as well as with the fingers and they make a full, deep sound that drives the beat of this dance music.

Look at the picture of women dancing the samba at the carnival in Rio de Janeiro. This carnival takes place every year. People compete for prizes awarded for the best costumes and the best dancers.

A pair of bongos

Drums from Japan

Listen to some traditional Japanese music. You will notice that each instrument or voice follows the same main tune, called the melody. Drums play an especially important part in supporting the melody. They provide a background of strong beats to keep the melody moving along to the right rhythm.

Gagaku

Gagaku is the official music played in the Japanese imperial court. It is one of the oldest forms of Japanese music.

A gagaku ensemble

There are usually three kinds of drums in the group of instruments, or ensemble, that plays gagaku music: the tsuri-daiko, the kakko, and the da-daiko. The tsuri-daiko hangs from a decorated wooden stand. You can see a tsuri-daiko in the picture below. It is played with two sticks.

The kakko rests on a low stand. The player hits both heads of the drum. The kakko is often used to play interesting rhythms. It has two membranes, one at each end, which are both beaten. The third instrument in the picture above is a gong.

Japanese theatre

A Japanese drum called the ko-tsuzumi is very important to the music of Japanese theatre. This drum is an hourglass shape and is painted black with gold decoration. It has two membranes made of horsehide stretched over iron rings. Small patches of paper are put on one of the membranes to make the sound more interesting. The two heads are bound together by a long cord which the player squeezes to make the skin tighter and so produce a higher note. The drum is held against the player's right shoulder. You can tell how skilled the drummer is by the colour of the cord on his drum. Orange-red cord is used by ordinary players, light blue by more advanced players and lilac by masters of the art.

A da-daiko from Japan

There is also a huge drum called a da-daiko which is used on special occasions. It is set on a special platform, in an elaborately decorated frame, with steps leading up to it. As you can see in the picture above, the drummer puts his left foot on the platform and his right foot on the upper step.

The ko-tsuzumi provides a rhythmic accompaniment to the drama, called 'No' theatre. In 'No' theatre, the actors wear masks and chant words to the accompaniment of music played by musicians on stage. A chorus of singers describes what is happening and comments on it.

A scene from a Japanese 'No' drama

From kettledrums to timpani

Kettledrums today are often played in pairs, with each drum sounding a different note. The Arab naqara are a pair of small kettledrums with wood or clay bodies. The membrane is laced onto the drum and beaten with small sticks. The membrane can be tightened by twisting a stick through the lacing to produce a higher note.

Nakers

Soldiers from Europe, called crusaders, went to the Middle East to fight in wars during in the 1100s and 1200s. There they heard the exciting sound of the Arab naqara, which were played by the enemy as a sign for the battle to begin. They were very impressed by the sound and many soldiers brought naqara back to Europe. In England, they were called nakers and came to be used in military battles, in dance music and in church processions.

A pair of naqara

A kettledrum was originally just a membrane stretched over a cooking pot – a very simple instrument. Then, gradually, people started making vessels especially for drums.

European nakers from the 1200s

Carried on horseback

Years ago, large kettledrums were played on horseback, or even on the back of a camel in Egypt and Arabia. A drum was suspended on each side of the player. A trumpet was often played at the same time. Kettledrums were sometimes even mounted on a carriage and taken into battle.

Tuning a kettledrum

Kettledrums can be tuned to change their note to a higher or lower sound. This is called changing the pitch of a note. To make them easy to tune accurately, a hoop was fixed round the top of the drum, with screws set round it. The screws could be tightened or loosened to change the tension of the membrane. Turning the screws to tune the drums in the middle of a performance is difficult.

Timpani

Modern orchestral kettledrums are known as timpani. The bowls are usually made from fibreglass and the membranes

from plastic. Timpani are much easier to tune. Many have a pedal that adjusts the tension of the membrane. Others have a handle at the top of the drum to do the same job. A range of sticks is used to play timpani, but perhaps the most common are felt-headed beaters like the ones in the picture below.

Kettledrums used in the Trooping the Colour ceremony in London

Timpani beaters

Orchestral drums

If you listen to *Peter and the Wolf* by the Russian composer Sergei Prokofiev you will hear the orchestral timpani and bass drum used very effectively. They mimic the sound of hunters shooting their guns in the forest. It is very realistic!

In a western orchestra, the drums are part of the percussion section, which is right at the back in the centre.

Playing orchestral timpani

In a large orchestra, you'll probably see a bass drum and a side drum. A side drum is a small drum fitted with snares, which you can read about on pages 120 and 121. You will also see between two and four kettledrums, called timpani. You can find out more about timpani on pages 116 and 117.

There may also be a tambourine, which you can read more about on pages 124 and 125, and a gong drum. The French composer Hector Berlioz asks for 16 kettledrums to be played by 10 drummers in one of his works!

The bass drum

The bass drum is the largest orchestral drum. It is so heavy that it is hung in a frame and can be hit from either side. The bass drummer uses many different beaters to give different effects. Its deep, booming stroke makes an unearthly sound. The biggest bass drum ever made measured about 4 metres across, but most bass drums are more likely to be about 1.3 metres across.

A bass drum

There is some interesting music for the orchestra's percussion section to play. Drums are no longer just for giving the beat. They've become musical instruments in their own right. The British composer Benjamin Britten wrote *The Young Person's Guide to the Orchestra*, in which the percussion instruments show just what they can do!

A bass drum beater

The snare drum

Look at the drum this soldier is playing as he marches along. It is called a snare drum. Snare drums are sometimes called side drums, because of the way soldiers carry them on their left side. They are made of wood or metal, with a plastic or calfskin membrane on both sides of the frame. There are eight or more strands of wire or nylon stretched tightly over the lower membrane.

These wire strands are called snares. When the drum is hit, the snares vibrate with the skin. This makes a biting, cracking sound. To stop the snares from vibrating, the drummer presses a lever at the side of the drum and this loosens the snares. Sometimes, drummers tuck a piece of cloth between the snares and the head to make sure there is no vibration.

A soldier marching
with a snare drum

A modern
snare drum

1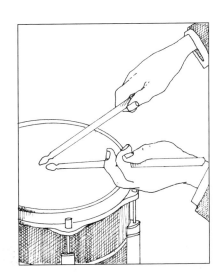

2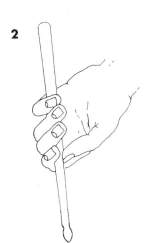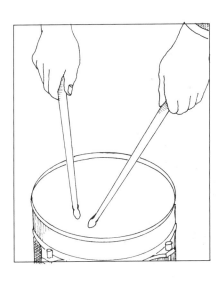

Roll your drum

So how do you play a snare drum as you march along on parade? First, you have to choose the right sticks. Heavy wooden sticks with large tips like the ones in the picture are best. They make a hard, strong sound as they hit the drum.

Now you must learn to hold the sticks correctly. There are different ways of doing this. The first picture above shows the traditional grip. This is the best grip to use when you're marching. You hold the stick between the two middle fingers. This is sometimes called the rabbit grip. Do you think it has the shape of a rabbit?

The second picture shows a different grip called the matched grip. This grip is useful to learn because many other drums are played like this. You hold the stick in your fist.

Then comes the playing. Drummers have to make sure they strike the centre of the drum with crisp, even strokes. But you can practice beating on any surface. Start with left stick (L) and right stick (R) taking it in turns – L R L R L R. Can you hear the rhythm? Lots of rhythms have names to help you get them right. You could do the 'Mummy/Daddy' roll, which goes like this: L L R R L L R R L L R R. Try it – it's not as difficult as you think!

1. The rabbit grip
2. The matched grip

Wooden drumsticks

The march of military bands

This picture, called *Music at the Customs House at Le Havre*, was painted by the French artist Raoul Dufy

You've already looked at the snare drum, which soldiers play on parade. But marching bands play lots of other drums, too. There's nothing like a good steady beat from a big bass drum to keep everyone in step. Military bands have kept weary soldiers marching to a regular beat for many years. They are exciting to watch, too. Perhaps you have stood and cheered while a large, colourful band like the one in the picture above marched by.

Drum and fife bands consist of fifes, which are small flutes, side drums, bass drum, cymbals and triangles. The shrill noise of the fifes dancing over the top of the beating percussion makes an exciting sound. Bigger military bands also contain brass instruments. The players' music is clipped onto small music holders called lyres. These are attached to the instruments so that the players can read the music as they march along.

Felt-headed bass drum beaters

The March King

The best-known composer of military marches is the American composer John Philip Sousa. He composed over one hundred marches and came to be known as the March King. Sousa played in the United States Marine band for five years and later became its bandmaster. Then in 1892, he started his own band, Sousa's Band.

You need long arms to hit the membranes on both sides with the felt-headed beaters, too! The bass drum is the instrument that sets the pace of the marching. Brisk marching speed is about 112 paces to the minute. You could time yourself to see if this is a comfortable speed. How many paces do you march in one minute?

A bass drum for marching

John Philip Sousa

Carrying a bass drum

Look at the bass drum in the picture on the right of this page. Bass drums made for marching can be more than 70 centimetres across so, as you can imagine, marching along with one strapped to your chest is not easy.

Beating the tambourine

'And Miriam the prophetess, the sister of Aaron, took a timbrel in her hand; and all the women went out after her with timbrels and dances'.

This is just one of many mentions of the timbrel, or tambourine, in The Bible. The tambourine is a very ancient instrument. Just like a simple drum, it has a frame with a single membrane stretched across it. But a tambourine often has metal discs attached to its frame. So a tambourine can be hit like a drum or shaken like a rattle.

Different tambourines

The pictures below show three different kinds of tambourine. The first is called a bendir and comes from Morocco. Can you see two strings stretched across it? These are snares, which work just like the snares on a snare drum. The second tambourine comes from Japan and the third from England.

Modern tambourines

Modern tambourines are a round wooden hoop with a plastic skin nailed or glued to one side. Most modern tambourines have pairs of metal jingle plates fixed around the edge.

1. A Moroccan bendir
2. A Japanese tambourine
3. A British tambourine from the 1800s

If you can find a tambourine to play, try these different playing methods:

- Hold it with one hand and hit it with the other.
- Shake it.
- Bang it against your knee or elbow.

Use a paper plate!

You can make your own tambourine from a plastic or paper plate. First, cut six holes in the edge of the plate in three groups of two. Now find your jingles. You can use metal rings, buttons or balls of aluminium foil. Fix the jingles you have chosen in pairs around the edge of the plate. Decorate your tambourine with paint and ribbons and you're ready to play a lively rhythm!

The modern drum kit

A drum kit being played on stage

wire
brushes

Look at this picture of a modern drum kit. Imagine yourself playing it on stage in front of a huge audience! You walk onto the stage to the accompaniment of whistles and screams from the audience. You bend over your drums, pick up the sticks and start to play. Your hands fly in all directions as you beat the snare drum, crash the cymbals and strike a kind of drum called a tomtom. Your feet are busy too – stamping on the bass drum pedal. As you finish, exhausted, the audience jumps to its feet to applaud. You're famous!

Drummers in a rock band or jazz group need tremendous energy as well as skill. They rush from drum to drum with amazing speed. Each hand and foot seems to be doing something different, but they are all precisely in time with each other.

A diagram of a modern drum kit

The basic kit

A basic drum kit consists of a whole range of equipment. The diagram below shows you each instrument. There's a pounding bass drum, shimmering snare drum, a pair of high-pitched tomtoms and a bigger tomtom that stands on the floor. You'll probably see three kinds of cymbals, too – a hi-hat cymbal which you operate by pressing a pedal, a free-swinging crash cymbal which you hit and a more rigid ride cymbal which gives good rhythm and accent.

The next time you listen to some rock music, listen carefully to the drums. Can you tell which kind of drum is playing?

1. bass drum
2. snare drum
3. tomtom
4. hi-hat cymbal
5. ride cymbal
6. crash cymbal
7. tomtom

— CHAPTER FOUR —

FLUTES, REEDS AND TRUMPETS

The wind rustling in the leaves of a tree can make sounds that are almost like music. People use their breath to make sounds, too, by blowing into a hollow object. Blowing into different kinds of objects makes different sounds.

The musical instruments you will see in this chapter are used for many different reasons. They may be used to play soft music for a sad occasion, or a thrilling march to cheer people up. In some of the pictures, you will see that people may dress in special clothes when they play their instruments.

It is fun experimenting to see what sounds you can make with your breath. In this chapter, you will find more simple projects for you to try so that you can hear exactly what wind instruments sound like.

Music from thin air

Take a deep breath and puff out your cheeks. Now blow out the air. Does the air make a sound as it rushes out of your mouth? It probably made a noise like rushing wind. You can make a louder sound with your breath if you blow into a tube.

Look around for some hollow objects. You could use a pen top, a hollow key, a straw or an empty bottle. Place the open end against your bottom lip. Push your top lip out slightly, then blow over the hole. You should be able to produce a strong whistle. Experiment by moving your lips until you hear a good sound.

You can also make a musical instrument using your breath and your hands. Cup your hands together as if you are holding a ball. Leave a small gap between your thumbs. Now rest your lips against the thumb joints and blow into your hands. Blow softly, then harder. Move your hands slightly until you get a rich sound like the hoot of an owl.

Musical vibrations

Do you know how blowing across a tube or into your hands makes a sound? When you blow into something hollow, the air inside the hollow container starts to vibrate.

Musicians from the Mehinack tribe in Brazil

Jaguar Playing a Shell Trumpet is an ancient wall painting from Mexico

Some of the vibrations escape from the container into the surrounding air and vibrate in waves, which we call sound waves. The waves travel to your ears, and these pick up the whistling sound.

People have been breathing into hollow objects to make musical sounds for thousands of years. The pictures on this page show that you can make music with almost any hollow object you find around you. The jaguar in the ancient Mexican wall painting is blowing into a large shell. And look back to the picture of musicians from the Mehinack tribe in Brazil. They are blowing into hollow pipes to make a musical sound.

Panpipes

According to ancient Greek legend, the god Pan had the horns, ears and legs of a goat and the face and body of a man. Pan often fell in love. One day, he was chasing a beautiful nymph called Syrinx. The gods took pity on Syrinx, and turned her into a reed so that she could escape from the god. Of course, Pan could not find her among so many reeds, but he cut one to remind him of Syrinx. Later, Pan made the reed into the first panpipes.

You can find panpipes in many parts of the world. They are a set of tubes of different lengths, joined together in a row. The tubes are usually blocked at the bottom.

A panpipes player from the Solomon Islands in the Pacific Ocean

Look at the picture of the musician from the Solomon Islands on the opposite page to see how to play the panpipes. As you blow, you move the panpipes backwards and forwards in front of your mouth to make different sounds.

Changing pitch

The panpipe tubes make a specific musical sound called a note. Because each tube is a different length, it sounds a different note. A short pipe gives a high note because there is less space for the air to vibrate in. We say that the length of each tube determines the pitch of the note it produces.

There is another way to change pitch. If you find an empty bottle you can demonstrate how to do it. First practise getting a note by blowing over the top. If you can't make a note straight away, change the shape of your lips or the position of the bottle. Or try strong, quick puffs of air. Now put some water in the bottle and blow again. What do you notice about the note? Put some more water in and try again. Each time

you add water, you reduce the space where the air can vibrate. So, each time, your note changes to a higher pitch.

Make your own panpipes

You can make your own panpipes from plastic tubing. Ask an adult to cut your tubing into about six pieces, with each piece slightly longer than the last. Then block the ends of the tubes with modelling clay. Wrap tape around the tubes to keep them together in a line. You may want to paint or decorate your pipes. If you have difficulty blowing a clear note on your pipes, try cutting a piece out of the end of each one.

The didgeridoo

An Aboriginal didgeridoo player

A long, deep, vibrating growl is followed by a gruff boom. A throttled scream is quickly replaced by explosive barks. High squeaks seem to mix with strange and muffled voices. And all the time there is the long, deep growl . . .

Listening to these sounds, you can imagine a magical conversation between animals, plants, wind, sky and the depths of the Earth. The music is hundreds of years old and you would hear it in Australia. The sounds are made on a didgeridoo. Say the word slowly, didg-er-i-doo. The word sounds like the music. The didgeridoo is played by the Aboriginal people on special occasions, to accompany dancing.

A special instrument

Everything about the didgeridoo is fascinating. As you can see from the picture above, it is a huge instrument! A didgeridoo can be several metres long. And it is made like no other instrument. First a branch is chopped from a eucalyptus tree and may be buried in a termite hill. The termites eat the soft wood inside the branch, leaving a hollow cylinder. This is taken out, cleaned, and sometimes decorated with patterns. The patterns usually take the form of dream-like animals, whose lives are described in Aboriginal myths. Didgeridoo music often expresses the voices of these mythical animals.

Blowing a continuous note

Didgeridoo music is a series of almost continuous notes. It seems as if there is no time for the musicians to breathe. So how do they manage? The Aboriginal player has developed a technique of continuous breathing. It takes an incredible amount of skill and practice. Take a deep breath through your nose. Breathe out steadily through your mouth. Just before you run out of breath, puff out your cheeks. And then – this is the difficult part – squeeze the air out of your cheeks and take a quick, deep breath through your nose at the same time. It seems impossible, but there is no magic to it – just technique and practice. But you don't just blow into the didgeridoo. It's really a kind of trumpet. You have to start the air vibrating inside by pursing your lips together as you blow.

Make your own didgeridoo

Make an instrument like a didgeridoo from a long cardboard tube, or a section of plastic tube used for drainpipes. Your tube needs to be about 1.5 metres long. Decorate the tube with bright patterns and start practising your continuous breathing! Once you can make the basic booming note, start experimenting. Make other sounds in the tube, like clicking, shouting, buzzing, croaking and humming. You probably won't master the skill of continuous breathing, but you will hopefully make some good sounds.

Whistles and duct flutes

Do you have a whistle at home? If you have, you know that it is a narrow pipe topped with a special part to blow into, called a mouthpiece. Just below the mouthpiece there is a narrow hole cut out of the pipe. When you blow into the mouthpiece, the air is aimed right onto the sharp edge of the hole. This makes it easier to blow a clear note. Whistles with this narrow hole cut into them are also known as duct flutes.

Duct flutes made from many different materials are found all over the world. The picture on the left shows a very old Chinese flute from the 900s which is made from bamboo. Most modern whistles, like the ones below, are made from metal, plastic or wood, but whistles can be made from bone or clay.

A Chinese duct flute player

Modern wood, plastic and metal whistles and recorders

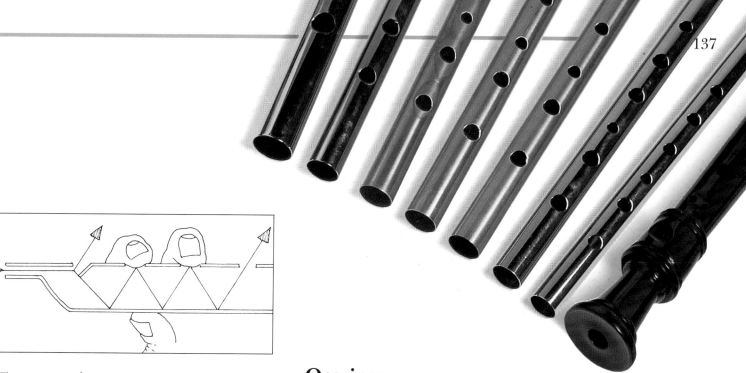

The passage of air inside a whistle with finger holes

Finger holes

You already know that to change the pitch of a note, you need to change the length of the tube. If you look at the diagram above, you will see that you can also change the pitch by adding finger holes to your tube. When you cover all the holes with your fingers, the tube is long. The air travels right down the length of the tube. When you cover only the lower holes, you are letting some of the air escape higher up the tube, so the tube is shorter and the note is higher. When you leave all the holes open, the air escapes out of the first hole it reaches and the note is higher still.

Different shapes

Not all whistles have long, straight tubes. Many are small and have a rounded shape. You may have a toy whistle with a round body and a straight piece to blow through. The referee's whistle on the right has a piece inside it that rotates to give a better sound.

Ocarinas

An ocarina is a small whistle with finger holes and a rounded body. Ocarinas come from Portugal and are popular in South America, where they are often made of clay moulded into interesting shapes like birds or people. The metal ocarina in the picture below comes from India. It has a chain attached to it so that you can wear it as a piece of jewellery.

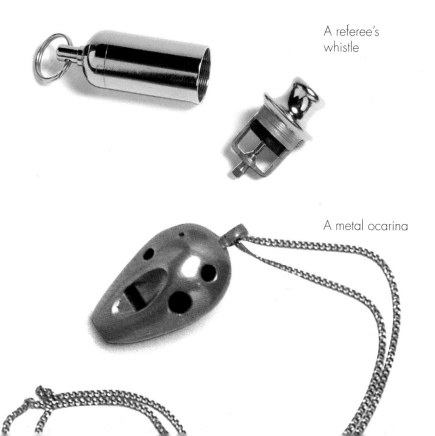

A referee's whistle

A metal ocarina

The story of the recorder

Arnold Dolmetsch

Late one evening in 1919, the Dolmetsch family joined a huge crowd of people waiting for a train at Waterloo Station in London. The family was returning home from a concert at which they had performed. Inside one of their bags was an old kind of duct flute called a recorder. At that time, recorders were rare instruments.

Seven-year-old Carl Dolmetsch put the bag down to rest his arms. Just then, the platform gates opened and the crowd of travellers surged forward. It was only when the train left the station that Arnold Dolmetsch discovered that his son had left the bag on the platform! The rare recorder was lost!

Are you wondering what happened to the recorder that was lost at Waterloo Station? Well, many years later it was found for sale in a junk shop. It was returned to the Dolmetsch family. And Carl, the seven-year-old who lost it? He grew up to be a talented musician and craftsman.

Arnold Dolmetsch set about making a new recorder in his workshop. Fortunately, he had made careful drawings and measurements of the old recorder. But it took a long time before Arnold was satisfied with the new instrument. He decided to make more recorders so that more people could learn to play them. The Dolmetsch family set up production in a factory. By the 1930s, the recorder was becoming as popular an instrument as it had been 200 years before.

A bass recorder

A group of musicians playing recorders in the 1600s

Sopranino, descant, treble and tenor recorders

In and out of favour

When the recorder was a fashionable instrument in Europe, composers wrote pieces of music especially for groups of recorder players. Then musical fashions changed. Composers began writing music for larger and larger orchestras. Audiences enjoyed listening to dramatic music in large concert halls. But the recorder was not suited to large places – it is best suited to small, intimate musical gatherings where its gentle sound can be appreciated. So people stopped playing and making recorders.

Today, the recorder is popular again, thanks largely to the Dolmetsch family. Recorders are not too expensive to buy or difficult to learn to play, so they are a good instrument for young people to choose. As you can see from the pictures on these pages, recorders come in different sizes. The large recorder is the bass, which plays the low notes. The smallest is the sopranino, which plays the highest notes.

The modern concert flute

This picture, *A Flute Concert at Friedrich the Great's Palace,* was painted by Adolphe von Menzel

Many flutes are held sideways across the player's mouth. They are called side-blown or transverse flutes. The player blows across the top of a blow hole to play the instrument. Flutes are an ancient kind of instrument which became popular in European concert music about 200 years ago. Early flutes, like the one in the picture on this page, had open holes along the pipe. You closed these with your fingers to change the pitch, just like a whistle. But early flutes were not easy to play because the fingering was complicated.

Making the fingering easier

A German jeweller and goldsmith called Theobald Boehm found an answer to this problem. Boehm was also an enthusiastic flute player and, around 1830, he concentrated his skills on improving the design of the concert flute. He wanted to make the complicated fingering easier. He invented an intricate system of keys, pads, hinges and levers to cover and uncover the holes. This made the fingering much easier.

A modern
concert flute

If you look at the pictures of concert flutes on this page, you will see how Boehm's system helps the flautist. It means that the player can press a lever and cover more holes than would be possible with the fingers. So the skilled flautist can play intricate music easily!

Different flutes

Some flautists prefer the sound of a wooden flute, but most concert flutes are now made from metal. There are two other kinds of metal flutes that are larger than the concert flute and play lower notes. They are called the bass flute and the alto flute and are usually played in quiet pieces of music, where their mellow sound can be heard best.

If you listen to *The Magic Flute*, an opera by the Austrian composer Wolfgang Amadeus Mozart, you will hear a concert flute played to great effect. It is used to mimic the sound of panpipes played by one of the main characters, Papageno.

The piccolo

The concert flute has a small relative. It is half the size and plays twice as high. It is called the piccolo flute, because piccolo means small in Italian. The piccolo has the same system of keys as the concert flute. You can hear the piccolo in the *Nutcracker Suite*, which was written by the Russian composer Peter Tchaikovsky.

An Indian
flautist

An orchestral
flautist

Natural trumpets and horns

A long trumpet from Tibet

Early trumpets and horns were made from natural materials in just the same way as early pipes. However, unlike pipes, trumpets and horns have a thin end to blow through and a thicker, cone-shaped end to carry the sound out into the air. It's often difficult to tell the difference between an early trumpet and an early horn. Trumpets are usually straight and horns are usually curved.

Early trumpets and horns were traditionally made from wood, animal horn, clay or bone. The long trumpet in the picture comes from Tibet. It is so long that the player has to rest the cone-shaped end in a forked tree to play it! The picture below shows a natural horn from Africa. It is made from an antelope's horn.

Musical shells

Long ago, people discovered that some giant seashells were excellent ready-made trumpets. In parts of India, a trumpet made from a conch shell like the one in the picture on the right is blown at Hindu festivals. In the Pacific islands of Fiji, the largest shell of all, called a triton, is blown to announce the opening of the local fish market.

A natural horn from Kenya

Sound cones

Try this experiment to see why cones are good for sound. Roll a large piece of paper or cardboard into a cone shape. Speak into the narrow end. Your voice will be made louder as it comes out of the wider, flared end. You have just made a megaphone. 'Mega' and 'phone' are Greek words meaning 'large-voice'. The cone-shaped end of a trumpet or horn, called the bell, pushes the sound forwards, making it louder. We say that the bell amplifies the sound.

A conch shell

Playing the trumpet

You have to use your lips to force air into a trumpet or horn and produce a good sound. Take a deep breath. Tighten your lips together. Now force the air out between your lips.

You will hear a sound like a buzzing bee. That's the air vibrating as it is pushed out between your lips. It is this vibration that makes the sound you recognize when horns and trumpets are played. Use your cardboard trumpets to blow some loud sounds or shout across the room to your friends!

The modern trumpet

In 1939, a rare silver trumpet with a long, straight tube was blown for the first time in 3,000 years. It was a tense and exciting moment. The effect was shattering. The trumpet broke into several pieces! The trumpet was one of two discovered in the tomb of the Egyptian Pharaoh Tutankhamun.

Tutankhamun's trumpet, like animal horns and conch shells, could only play a few notes. It was probably used for signalling or for playing fanfares on special occasions. Have you ever heard the thrilling sound of a fanfare? In Europe they are still played on straight trumpets for grand ceremonial occasions.

A modern trumpet

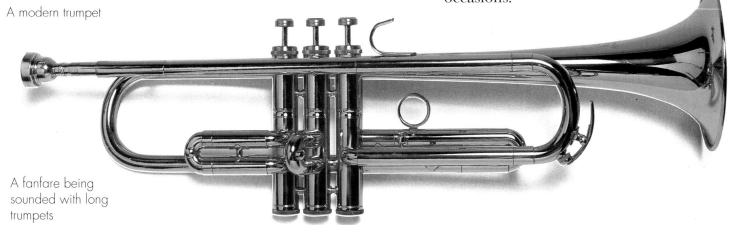

A fanfare being sounded with long trumpets

Folded tubes

The modern metal trumpet developed from long trumpets like Tutankhamun's. Straight trumpets like the ones used to play fanfares have an extraordinarily long tube. You can imagine how this would get in the way, especially in a band or orchestra. To overcome this problem, modern trumpets have been folded up! Look at the picture of a modern trumpet above. You can see how long it would be if the tubing were stretched out. If you measured it, you would find that the tubing is 1.4 metres long! Modern trumpets also have a detachable mouthpiece, which helps to carry the vibration from the player's lips into the tubing more effectively.

Keys

Around 1800, trumpets were developed that had keys, like the ones on flutes. Many more notes could be played on these instruments. A very famous piece of music was written for a trumpet like this. The composer was Joseph Haydn, an Austrian. It is called Haydn's *Trumpet Concerto*. It's still very popular with trumpet players today.

How trumpet valves work

Valves

In 1815 an even better system was invented to improve the range of sound the trumpet could make. Three valves were added to the tubing. The diagram shows you how they work. When the player presses down on a valve, an extra length of tubing is opened. This makes a longer column of air and sounds a lower note. When the valve is released, the tubing closes again. At last the trumpet was able to join in and play any tune that had been written.

The trumpet certainly makes a stirring sound! It is probably most effective when it is played with feeling by a soloist like the American musician in the picture below.

A trumpet player at the Mardi Gras celebration in New Orleans in the United States of America

Modern brass instruments

The modern trumpet belongs to a family of metal instruments that we call brass instruments. The other main members of the family are the tuba, the trombone and the French horn. When these instruments play together in an orchestra, we call them the brass section.

The tuba

The French composer Maurice Ravel decided to arrange a piece of music, *Pictures at an Exhibition* by Modeste Mussorgsky, for an orchestra. One of the 'pictures' was of an ox cart lumbering along a muddy lane. He chose a tuba to represent the sound of the ox cart.

An Australian tuba player

Lengthy tubing

The picture on the left shows you just what a large instrument the tuba is. Normally, tubas play the lowest notes of all the brass instruments in the orchestra. So you can imagine how much tubing it has – at least 3.75 metres! In the early 1900s, an enormous tuba was built in America. The length of its tubing was 10.36 metres! It was so large, a person could disappear inside the bell. Tubas have the same valve system as trumpets.

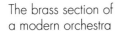

The brass section of
a modern orchestra

The trombone

A long time ago, the trombone was
called the sackbut. It was named after an
old French word 'saqueboute' meaning
'pull-push'. Instead of having valves to
change the length of the tube, like other
brass instruments, trombones have a
moving length of tubing called a slide.
As you play the trombone, your arm
does a 'push-pull' action to move the
slide in and out, making the passage of
air longer and changing the pitch of the
note you play.

The French horn

Even though it is a smaller instrument,
the French horn has about the same
length of tubing as a tuba. The tubing is
curled in a tight circle. You can make an
instrument similar to the French horn.
You need about 4 metres of rubber hose,
with a plastic funnel. Use a brass
instrument mouthpiece to blow into.
Curl the hose around and tuck it under
your arm to play it. Remember to
tighten or slacken your lips as you blow.

Brass bands

Can you imagine the sound of lots of brass instruments all playing together? Think of a band of musicians turning the corner and marching down your street! They are playing trombones, trumpets and horns, not to mention cornets and tubas, as well as drums and crashing cymbals. You would probably see the trombone players first. They often lead a parade, so that there is plenty of space for their long slides to move in and out.

A trombone

A cornet

Special instruments

Brass bands have several of their own special brass instruments, which you wouldn't normally see in an orchestral brass section. One of these is the cornet.

As you can see from the picture on the left, a cornet looks like a small trumpet. But cornets make a much softer and sweeter sound. That's why they are used in brass bands instead of the more piercing trumpet.

The horns, too, are different from the horns in the orchestra. In 1845, a Belgian instrument maker named Adolphe Sax made a family of instruments called saxhorns, especially for use in brass bands. They are not called saxhorns now – their names are flugelhorn, tenor horn, baritone horn and the largest one is the euphonium.

A Salvation
Army band

Playing together

Since the middle of the 1800s, brass bands have become an especially popular form of entertainment in many countries. In the United States, town parades always feature a brass band, usually with marching majorettes.

In the northern parts of England, many towns and villages have their own bands, and many more are found in workplaces like factories and coal mines. Contests are held to find out which band is the best.

Since ancient times, armies have used brass instruments to carry out special tasks. They could be used for sending signals, such as 'march forward' or 'retreat'. Their music would also keep up the soldiers' spirits and help them to march in time together into battle. Of course, army bands don't do this now, but they still play for special occasions and in parades.

Over a hundred years ago, in England, a man named William Booth started a different kind of army. His was not a military army, but a religious one. He called his religious group the Salvation Army. William Booth loved brass bands and so he started his own to attract crowds to his open-air religious meetings. By the time he died in 1912, Salvation Army bands were playing all over the world.

A marching band from England

Reeds

Have you ever made a shrill sound by blowing over a blade of grass held between your thumbs? As the blade of grass vibrates, it makes the air vibrate in sound waves. We hear the waves as a sharp buzzing sound.

Some instruments use a device that works in a similar way to the blade of grass to make a musical sound. We call them reed instruments. Reed instruments have a mouthpiece which contains one or two strips of cane, plastic or fibreglass. These strips are called reeds.

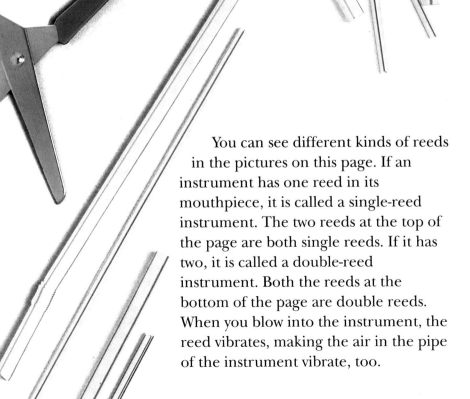

You can see different kinds of reeds in the pictures on this page. If an instrument has one reed in its mouthpiece, it is called a single-reed instrument. The two reeds at the top of the page are both single reeds. If it has two, it is called a double-reed instrument. Both the reeds at the bottom of the page are double reeds. When you blow into the instrument, the reed vibrates, making the air in the pipe of the instrument vibrate, too.

Double reeds

The two reeds of a double-reed instrument make an extra sound because they vibrate against each other. You can see how this works using a straw. Cut two slits in one end, then cut across the slits to make a wedge shape. Put the cut end of the drinking straw just behind your teeth, then close your lips around the straw. Squeeze the cut ends together with your teeth and tongue. Blow hard. You should get a vibrating sound. Now cut a short length off the other end of the straw and blow again. What do you notice about the pitch of the note? It should sound higher.

In a double-reed instrument, two pieces of thin reed are carefully cut, shaped and tied together. The reeds are then fixed to the instrument. When you blow through the reeds, they flutter rapidly together. This makes the air in the instrument vibrate.

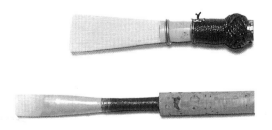

The shawm

Shawms like the one being played in the picture below are loud, double-reed instruments whose raucous, penetrating sound is ideal for events like military parades and other ceremonies. Shawm players often puff out their cheeks for continuous breathing, just like the Aboriginal didgeridoo musicians. Shawm music is popular throughout the Islamic world. Shawms are also found in Africa, Europe and south east Asia.

A shawm player
from Chad in Africa

Orchestral reeds

There is a children's story from Russia about a boy called Peter, his grandfather, a cat, a bird, a duck, a wolf and some hunters. The story is special because it is told not just in words but in music, too. Each character is matched to an instrument of the orchestra. Whenever you hear the instrument, you picture the character it represents. Three of the characters are played by reed instruments – the clarinet, the oboe and the bassoon. These are the three main reed instruments in the orchestra.

The clarinet

The sleek, black cat is played by the clarinet, which is a single-reed instrument. You can see a picture of one on the left. The clarinet can jump easily from high to low notes, play very loudly or very quietly, and move fast or slow. The low sounds are rich and velvety, the high ones piercing and bright.

The oboe

The quacking duck is played by the oboe. The oboe can move very quickly from sound to sound, too. Its low sounds are raucous and reedy, its high ones thin and penetrating. This is possible because the oboe has two reeds which vibrate against each other, exactly like the shawm. The instrument on the right is an oboe.

A clarinet plays the sound of the cat

An oboe plays the quacking duck

Peter's grandfather
is played by
the bassoon

A bassoon player
in an orchestra

The bassoon

The bassoon's tubing is four times as long as that of the oboe. The tube is so long, in fact, that it is folded, like most of the brass instruments. As you can see from this picture, the bell points upwards above the player's head rather than down. It makes a lower sound than the other reed instruments. People say that some of its notes can sound like the human voice. Perhaps that's why the bassoon plays the voice of Peter's grumbling grandfather.

The story and its music were written in 1936 by a Russian composer named Sergei Prokofiev. It is called *Peter and the Wolf*. Perhaps you can find a recording of it and listen to what happens in the story. Do you think Prokofiev chose the right instruments for his characters?

All the characters
from *Peter and
the Wolf*

Jazz

Jazz is a mixture of many different kinds of music. Although jazz is now played nearly all over the world, its true 'home' is the United States of America. This is where jazz began almost 100 years ago. Early jazz was created by black-American people, the descendants of slaves who were brought from Africa. Their jazz was a combination of a kind of sad folk music called blues, mixed with melodies and rhythms from African music, church music, brass band music and from popular dances.

This early music is sometimes called Dixieland Jazz. 'Dixie' is an area of the southern states of the United States. A band playing this traditional jazz is often made up of brass instruments like a cornet and trombone, with perhaps a clarinet.

Improvised jazz

Jazz is different from most other kinds of music. It is mostly improvised. This means that musicians make up the music as they play.

A modern American jazz band

The American jazz
saxophone player
Charlie Parker

Improvised music works best with small groups, where the musicians can easily follow each other. But large orchestras can play jazz, too. These big bands were a popular form of entertainment between the 1930s and the 1950s. One famous band leader was Duke Ellington. He wrote his own music for his band and arranged it so that each musician knew what to play. Then during the performance, certain musicians played improvised solos on their own. The sound of big-band music helped jazz become known to a larger audience and become popular in many countries outside the United States.

The saxophone

It was during the time of the big bands that the saxophone became such an important jazz instrument. Compared to other brass instruments, the saxophone is quite new. It is a single-reed instrument and was invented by Adolphe Sax, who you read about on page 148, about 150 years ago.

If you look at the picture of a saxophone on the right, you will see that it has a system of keys, like the keys of a concert flute. The saxophone, or sax as it's often called, is a very expressive instrument. Players develop their own personal style of playing. You can often recognize a particular musician after hearing only a few notes. A saxophone player with a good technique can play loudly or softly.

One of the most famous saxophone players was the American musician Charlie Parker. He helped start a new style of improvised jazz called be-bop. This jazz can be difficult music to listen to, but it is powerful and exciting.

A saxophone

Bagpipes

This painting, by the Flemish artist Pieter Breughel the Elder, is called *Peasant Dance*

Look at this painting of people noisily enjoying themselves. It was painted 400 years ago by a Flemish artist named Pieter Breughel. A man and woman are running to join in the dancing at a village festival. Around a table sit three men arguing. Children play. And what is the instrument that is playing music to accompany the lively dancing? It's an instrument called the bagpipes.

This instrument originated in the Middle East, but many parts of Europe and Asia now have their own particular form of bagpipes. The most famous type are the highland pipes, which originally came from Scotland. These impressive instruments, with their loud, forceful sound, are now played by musicians in many different countries around the world.

Bagpipes from Russia

How to play the bagpipes

Bagpipes are very difficult instruments to play well. There are so many different things for the musician to do. The player has to blow hard into the bag and then squeeze it to push the air back out. At the same time, he fingers the holes in the pipe, or chanter, to play the tune. And then there are the drones, those long pipes that rest on the musician's shoulder. The drones make a continuous note which accompanies the tune played on the chanter.

Hidden reeds

Bagpipes are reed instruments, but you can't see the reeds. They are fixed in the ends of the pipes inside the bag. Usually a chanter has a double reed, like a shawm or an oboe. The drones generally have a single reed, like a clarinet. The bag acts as a reservoir for air. It is nearly always made of sheep's or goat's skin. You can clearly see the skin of the folk bagpipes in the picture above, although it is often covered with cloth. Because the air in the bag makes the reeds

vibrate, the player can breathe and still produce a continuous sound.

Not all bagpipes produce loud sounds. The Northumbrian 'small-pipes', shown in the picture below, play enchanting music with a much gentler sound. They are not blown by mouth, but by bellows, which the player pumps by moving the arm up and down.

Kathryn Ticknell, a Northumbrian 'small-pipes' player from England

Free reeds

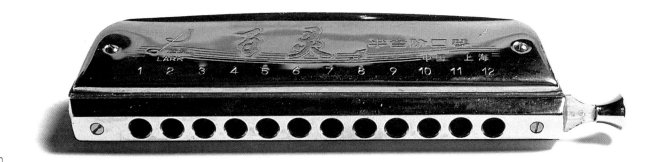

A modern mouth organ

Take a close look at the instrument in the picture above. It is called a mouth organ, or harmonica. This kind of instrument was invented in Europe about 150 years ago. Can you think how the mouth organ makes a musical sound? Each tiny hole has two metal reeds next to it, one short and one longer. When you blow into the holes, the reeds vibrate. Short reeds make high notes, longer ones make lower notes. These are called 'free reeds' because they are free to vibrate up and down.

Playing the mouth organ

You hold the instrument so that the low notes are to your left. Try to blow just one single note by blocking the other holes to the side with your tongue. What happens when you suck? If you don't move your mouth, you will hear a different note. That's because you activate the second reed by sucking instead of blowing. You can see how it works by looking at the diagram.

The sheng from China

A Chinese sheng

Mouth organs have been played in China for thousands of years, where they are called shengs. As you can see from the picture on the left, shengs are very different from the European mouth organ. They have long pipes and each has a free reed inside. The sheng player blows and sucks air through a wind box to play the same note, with different pitches. The reeds vibrate when the holes are closed.

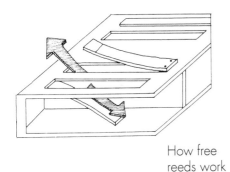

How free reeds work

The American folk and rock musician Bob Dylan

Famous players

Some harmonicas are designed to play very complicated music. One man who became a virtuoso, or expert, on the harmonica was the American musician Larry Adler. He wanted to show that the harmonica deserved to be taken seriously as a musical instrument. The English composer Ralph Vaughan Williams wrote a piece of harmonica music especially for Larry Adler.

The mouth organ is also an ideal instrument for folk and blues music. It has a mournful sound that goes very well with a solo voice. The famous American folk singer Bob Dylan is well known for his mouth organ playing. Can you see the frame he wears to support his mouth organ? This frees his hands so that he can play the guitar and the mouth organ at the same time!

The melodica

The instrument in the picture below is a melodica. It is a new kind of free-reed instrument, invented only 30 years ago. The body is made of plastic. The metal reeds are controlled by a tiny keyboard. Melodicas are cheap to buy and easy to play.

A melodica

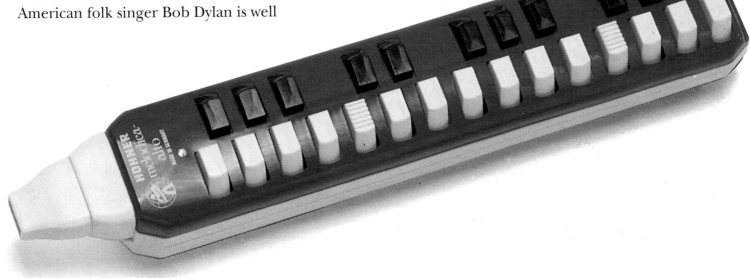

Squeeze boxes

Just like the mouth organ, a squeeze box makes music using free reeds. The largest squeeze boxes are the accordion and the melodeon. Musicians usually carry these instruments on a strap around their shoulder to support the weight. Squeeze boxes have three important parts. They are the reeds, the keys or buttons and the bellows.

The bellows

The bellows are like a folded-up bag. The player opens and closes the bellows-bag with a push-and-pull action of the left arm. When the bellows are opened, air is sucked in and when the bellows are shut, the air is pushed out.

Playing the accordion at the Moscow folk festival in Russia

A melodeon

The air flows past the reeds, making them vibrate and creating a sound. The player's right hand picks out the tune on a keyboard. The left hand presses groups of buttons at the other end of the bellows. On some accordions, there are as many as 120 buttons which can be pressed to sound chords. Each key and button controls a valve that supplies air to a reed or set of reeds.

The harmonium

You have to be athletic to play the harmonium! It is a free-reed instrument with a keyboard like a piano. It works in the same way as a harmonica and an accordion, the difference being in the way the bellows are operated. To play the harmonium, you have to pump two large pedals at the base of the instrument with your feet to fill the bellows with air. If you stop pumping, no noise will come out of the instrument. Small harmoniums that are pumped by hand are popular in India.

A harmonium player from India

Changing the sound

The keys and buttons on an accordion are called registers and complers. They can change the sound of the instrument completely. They allow one accordionist to sound like a whole group of musicians!

The concertina

Some squeeze boxes have different kinds of keyboards. A concertina is smaller than an accordion and is held in the hands with straps at each end. Both ends are hexagonal-shaped and both ends have buttons. Concertinas were traditionally used at sea to accompany sailors' songs called sea shanties.

The organ

This picture shows a beautiful example of one of the largest of all wind instruments. It is an organ. Just imagine how much air is needed to make all these organ pipes sound!

Of course, people don't blow into organ pipes. Mechanical gadgets such as bellows and electric motors are used. In the very first organs, made in Ancient Greece and Rome over 2,000 years ago, water was used to force air through the pipes. The first organ was called a hydraulis, from the Greek words for 'water' and 'pipe'. According to writers of the time, the sound was so powerful it could be heard many miles away and the players had to plug their ears!

A few hundred years later, bellows took over the job of supplying the air. A monk living in England about 1,000 years ago tells of a gigantic organ with 400 pipes that sounded like thunder. It had 26 bellows and needed 70 people to work them! Today, only one musician is needed to play an organ even as large as this one.

The sound of pipes

The types of organs that still exist today were first used about 300 years ago in European churches. They are able to imitate the sounds of many instruments of the orchestra – the violin, flute, trumpet, oboe and clarinet for example. Some of the pipes have ducts cut into them and work just like a recorder. Other pipes have metal reeds that vibrate like those of the clarinet.

An organ pipe

Small organs

Not all organs were as big as this. The small, sweet-sounding portative organ was popular during the 1400s and 1500s in Europe. It could be held and played at the same time by one person. One hand worked the bellows and the other hand played the keyboard in the same way as the Indian harmonium player on page 161.

A portative organ

An organ's keyboard and stops

Choosing the sound

The organist chooses different sounds by pressing down or pulling out stops to open and close the pipes. Most organs have two keyboards, called manuals, for the hands and one keyboard for the feet, called a pedalboard. Each keyboard controls a separate set of pipes. The organist plays tunes on the keyboards and operates the stops at the same time. Eyes, ears, hands, feet and brain all have to work together to control such a complicated machine.

One of the greatest composers for the organ was Johann Sebastian Bach. He lived and worked in Germany in the 1700s. When he was young he once walked over 300 kilometres to hear a famous organist play. Perhaps this inspired him to write the organ music for which he became famous and which is still popular today.

Electrifying music

An electric
Hammond organ

Electric organ

The American inventor Laurens Hammond invented the electric organ in the 1930s. The electric organ looks just like an ordinary pipe organ, but doesn't work unless it's switched on. When the keys are pressed, electric signals are made. The signals go to a pre-amplifier, where they are made stronger, then to an amplifier and then come out of the loudspeaker as musical notes. It sounds just like the real thing!

Electric pianos, like the one in the picture below, are popular with rock and pop musicians. It's a lot easier to carry a small electric keyboard around than a piano. The next time you hear some pop music on the keyboard, see if you can hear whether it's a real or electric piano.

An electronic
keyboard

When is an organ not an organ? Perhaps when it's electric. In 1937, the members of the Federal Trade Commission in the United States couldn't make up their minds. Could an electric organ really be called an organ? To decide the matter, they set up a test. One hidden player played a pipe organ and another player played an electric organ. An audience listened and tried to decide which was which. They couldn't tell the difference between the two!

A musician playing
a synthesizer

The synthesizer

Shortly after the electric organ was invented, the synthesizer was developed. This machine produces a range of electronic sounds. It can sound like an organ or a piano, and it can reproduce sounds like the hooting of a car horn or the ringing of a telephone. Synthesizers don't always look like a keyboard. You might see some that need to be blown like a woodwind instrument!

Synthesizers give musicians complete freedom to experiment with sounds. They can perform any amount of complicated music single-handedly. Composers such as Karlheinz Stockhausen and Jean-Michel Jarre have written scores for electronic instruments.

Of course, you don't have to be a skilled composer to play electronic instruments – let the instrument do the work. In fact, playing a synthesizer can be like having your own private orchestra. You can play pop, jazz or even your own symphony.

Unusual wind instruments

A serpent

Serpent

It is obvious how this instrument got its name! It looks like a snake, but it is not used by snake charmers. The serpent was first made about 400 years ago in France but is seldom played today. If the serpent were straightened out, it would be about 2.5 metres long. Remember the brass instruments whose tubing was so long it had to be folded up? A similar thing has happened with the serpent but it is made of wood, which is difficult to bend. So it's made in short hollowed-out sections that are glued together. They are then covered with leather to seal the joints and stop the air from escaping.

An Indian snake charmer

Snake charmer's pipe

Can snakes hear? Can they dance? Snake charmers in India would have us believe so. They play a pipe called a tiktiri. It is made from two cane pipes, each with a single reed. The pipes are fitted into one end of a hollowed-out dried vegetable called a gourd. The player blows through a hole in the other end.

The sound is loud and shrill, but the snakes can't hear it – they don't have ears. So why do they rise out of the basket and sway or dance? The reason is that they don't like the movements of the snake charmer and rise up in anger. Perhaps they can feel the vibrations from the music, too.

Nose flute

Blow through your mouth. Then blow through your nose. Which feels stronger? Even though you get a more powerful sound by blowing a flute the normal way, through your mouth, some people use their nostrils. In countries like Polynesia, where nose flutes are commonly played, the people think that air from the nose contains a person's soul and so has more magical power than breath from the mouth. Nose flute players like the Brazilian musician in the picture below believe that their music has special significance. Nose flute players usually block one nostril and blow into the flute with the other.

Bullroarer

You can make your own unusual wind instrument with a thin, rectangular piece of wood about 15 centimetres long and 2 centimetres wide. The exact shape and size are not too important. Ask an adult to help you make a small hole at one end. Tie one end of a long piece of smooth string into the hole. Make sure it is tied on very firmly.

Hold the string about half a metre from the wood. Twist the wood with your other hand. The string will start to wind up tightly. Now move into a large open space, and quickly swing the wood on the end of the string round and round your head. You will hear an unusual roaring noise. You have made an instrument called a bullroarer.

An Indian from the Amazon rain forest in Brazil playing a nose flute

— CHAPTER FIVE —

MAKING MUSIC

You have seen in this book that there are three sides to music — composing, performing and listening. You do not have to be a brilliant musician to enjoy doing any of these!

In this section you can read about some of the well-known composers who have written some great music. Composers write music that reflects their own ideas, and they sometimes write it down in unusual ways, as you will see.

Anyone can listen to music. But the more you know about the music you hear, the more fun you can get out of going to a concert. And by learning to play an instrument yourself, you will have a greater enjoyment of the wonderful world of music.

Recording music

A gramophone used to play music in the early 1900s

You want to listen to music played by your favourite drummer. So what do you do? You switch on a tape or CD player. But have you ever thought how the music got onto that tape or CD?

One hundred and fifty years ago, there was no recorded music at all. If you wanted to hear music you had to go to a concert or play it yourself. The earliest recordings were played on gramophones and sounded scratchy and muffled.

Music is usually recorded in a recording studio. Musicians play and sing into microphones and these turn the sound into electric signals. The signals are registered on a multi-track tape recorder. The best recording is done digitally, which means that the electric signals are coded by a computer.

Then the engineers and performers listen to the tape and decide if any parts of the music need to be recorded again. A balance engineer can alter the balance to make sure that none of the musicians is playing too loud or too soft. You can see the range of equipment the engineers use in the picture on the next page. When everyone is happy with the recording, the tape editor cuts the tape and fits together the best parts. Then a master tape is produced.

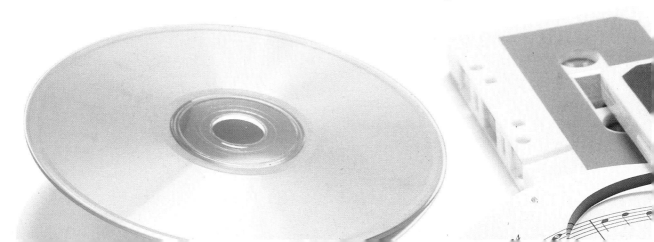

Today, you can listen to music on a CD or DAT (Digital Audio Tape), where the sound is so realistic it is as if the musicians are playing in the room with you. CDs, or compact discs, come from a master tape too, but this time a digitally recorded tape is used. A special beam of light called a laser beam cuts grooves into a master disc, from which the CDs are made. But don't forget that there's nothing like the excitement of hearing your favourite drummer performing at a live concert. It's hard to record atmosphere onto tape!

Recording music in the studio

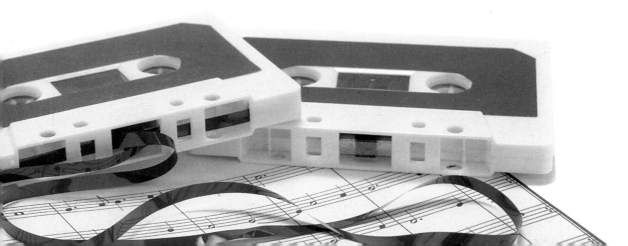

CDs and tapes

Going to a concert

An orchestra playing at a classical concert

Going to any kind of musical concert is exciting. But concerts vary according to the type of music that will be played. So when you buy your ticket, how will you know what to expect?

A classical concert

If you are lucky enough to be able to listen to a well-known orchestra playing in a large concert hall, your ticket might be expensive. You might even have to dress up for the occasion! It's a good idea to listen to a recording of the music beforehand. Then you will know about the music and be able to appreciate it.

The orchestra will start to play at a set time and you must be in your seat ten minutes or so before this. You already know that the players in the orchestra must tune their instruments before starting to play. Once the concert is about to begin, the conductor attracts the attention of the orchestra — usually by tapping on the rostrum and raising the baton. Some classical concerts start with an overture. The orchestra plays an opening piece which helps to set the scene for the music to follow.

Then the main part of the concert begins. If you are listening to a long piece of music, you will probably find it is divided into short sections. These are called movements. Remember that it is usual to clap only at the end of a piece. So even if you are particularly impressed by a performance, don't clap until other people do — you might put the musicians off. You will be able to express your appreciation by clapping loudly at the end of the concert!

A rock concert

How different is a rock concert to a classical concert? The answer is very different! To begin with, you may not even have a seat, especially if you are attending an open air concert. The audience often stands up or sits on the ground — so it's not necessary to dress up for a rock concert. You might be amazed at how many people there are at the concert, too. Rock concerts often attract huge audiences of ten thousand people, or more.

Rock bands need to tune their instruments just as members of an orchestra do. But if the instruments are electrical, they may be tuned by engineers. Once the band appears on stage, you'll notice the real difference to a classical concert. The audience cheers, claps, stamps and sings along! In fact, you may not notice a gap between the pieces of music at all.

Of course, there are many other kinds of concert and many different places where concerts are put on. Folk music or jazz concerts may take place in small halls or rooms so that the musicians don't have to use microphones. Even the busker or one man band who plays in the street in your town is giving a concert. But all concerts need an audience, so it is up to you to make sure you take the opportunity to listen.

The stage and audience at a large rock concert

What every performer needs

Every performer needs a few simple pieces of equipment, if nothing else, to give a successful performance. It is well worth spending a little time beforehand to make sure of a worthwhile result.

A metronome

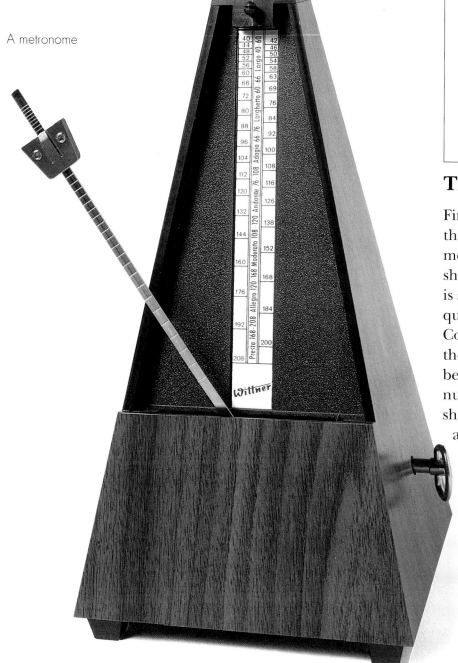

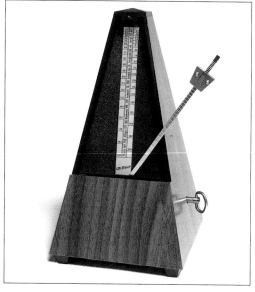

The metronome

First make sure you play your music at the right speed. A machine called a metronome tells you what the speed should be. But how fast is fast? How slow is slow? It's not always easy to decide how quickly a piece should be played. Composers often give an indication of the speed by putting numbers at the beginning of a piece of music. These numbers show how many beats there should be in a minute, from a slow 40 to a whizzing 208. The metronome helps you know exactly how quickly to play. You set the metronome by positioning a weight against the marks on a bar until it points to the chosen speed. Then you set it ticking, like a clock. Each tick represents one beat.

The tuning fork

When you play an instrument, especially in a group, you have to make sure that every instrument plays each note at the same pitch. The pitch must not vary from instrument to instrument, or the music will be out of tune.

Sound is caused by vibrations of air. Scientists measure pitch by counting how many vibrations a sound makes in one second. Low notes have few, slow vibrations, and high notes have many, fast ones.

The note A, which many instruments use to tune from, is fixed at 440 vibrations per second. This is known as concert pitch. Instruments tuned to concert pitch will sound the same all over the world. You can get the correct pitch of a note from a device called a tuning fork. This is a piece of metal that sounds a precise note when it is struck gently on a surface. You may also have seen an electrical tuner like the one in the picture. This picks up the sound waves from the note you play and shows them on a screen.

Once you've fixed the pitch of one note, you can match the pitch of all the others to it. Now you can put your music on a music stand and the performance can begin. Good luck!

An electrical tuner

A tuning fork

Learning to play an instrument

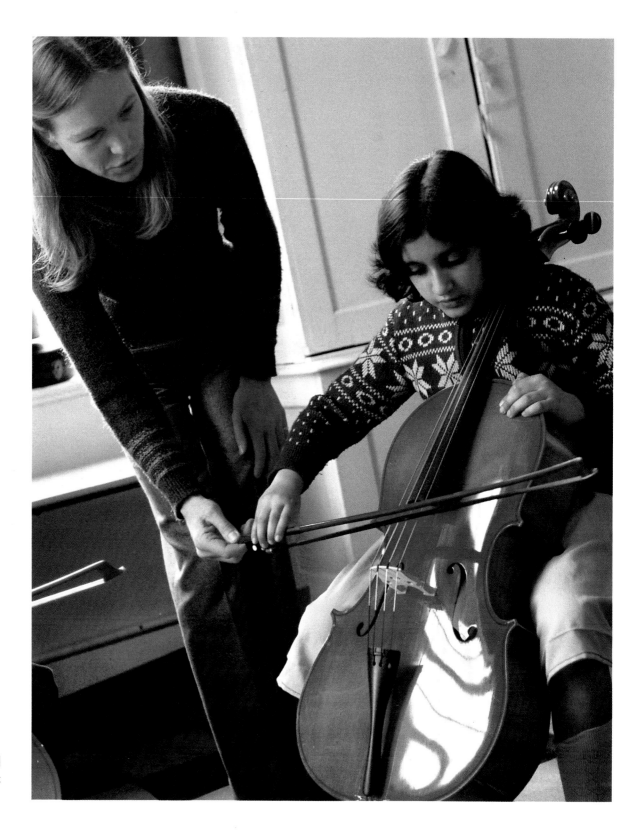

A cello teacher and her pupil at a music lesson

You have read about a great number of instruments in this book. Would you like to play any of them? If so, you first need to select the instrument you will play. Your choice may be limited because some instruments will be difficult to find. Perhaps you already know where there is a piano you can play but finding a tube fiddle might be more difficult. Remember that you don't have to buy the instrument you want to play. Most will be very expensive to buy and there is no point in spending money on an instrument and then finding out that you don't enjoy playing it! It is a good idea to rent the instrument at first.

Find a teacher

It is possible to learn to play an instrument on your own, and many famous musicians are self-taught. But this is a hard way to learn. The best way is to have lessons from a good music teacher. You may be able to have individual lessons at school, or to arrange private lessons in your own time. A music teacher will be able to pass on a great deal of knowledge to you, point out mistakes and help you improve your playing. If you get on well your teacher will probably encourage you to take examinations to measure your progress.

Playing with others

Once you have reached a certain standard, you will probably enjoy playing your instrument with other musicians in a musical group. Perhaps you will even be invited to join a youth orchestra. But even if your playing is just adequate, don't worry. As long as you enjoy your music, nothing else matters!

Practising the guitar

Practise hard

Learning an instrument is hard work. You will have to practise until all the basic aspects of playing the instrument come naturally and quickly. This may mean at least an hour of practice every day. But it is only when you have learned the basics off by heart like this, that you will be able to develop your own style of playing and perhaps develop a real talent.

Writing music

An illustrated music score from the 800s

Sharing music

We call people who write music composers, because they make up, or compose, music. They write down their musical ideas so that musicians can play the music accurately. They are using music as a form of language to share their thoughts and feelings with the people who hear their music. Composers work in different ways. Some composers use a piano to play parts of the music they hear in their heads before they write it down. Some write many versions, or drafts, of a single piece of music, changing it over and over again until it is absolutely right.

In the 800s monks invented a way of writing music down. Before that time all music was learned by heart, or it was forgotten as soon as it had been played. Look at this piece of music, which was written in 1420. You can see that it is not that different from modern written music. You might think that the colours and decoration make it more attractive!

A written piece of music like this one is called a score. Scores can be written for just one instrument or voice, or for many instruments or voices. If there is more than one part, they are written one above the other.

We know that the German composer Ludwig van Beethoven wrote like this because many of his draft scores still exist today.

Other composers work completely in their heads and write down their music only when it is finally shaped. The Austrian composer Wolfgang Amadeus Mozart worked in this careful way.

The German composer Ludwig van Beethoven

A modern score

Today, modern composers are writing scores in different, new ways. Composers such as Karlheinz Stockhausen from Germany use diagrams and pictures as well as notes to convey their musical ideas. This means that a modern score can look quite different from a traditional one. Part of this Stockhausen composition is in the shape of a triangle. Have you ever seen a piece of music like it?

But no matter how different scores can look, they all serve the same purpose. They tell the musicians what notes to play, the speed to play them and even the mood the composer wants to convey. A written score allows the musician to achieve a performance that is as close as possible to the music originally imagined by the composer.

A modern composition by the German composer Karlheinz Stockhausen

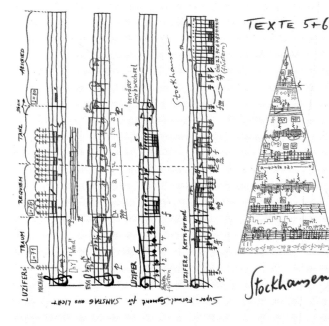

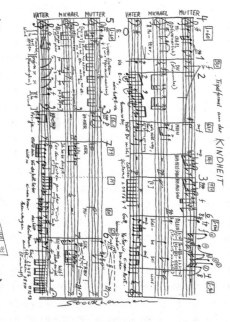

Composers' biographies

Johann Sebastian Bach (1685-1750)

Bach is considered to be the greatest German composer of his time. He was born in Eisenach into a musical family, and was brought up by his brother, who was an organist. At the age of 18, Bach went to work for the brother of the reigning Duke as a musician. In 1708, Bach became organist and chamber musician to the Duke of Weimar. He had to compose a church cantata for every month of the year. In 1717, he was appointed court musical director to Prince Leopold. And in 1723, he took charge of the music of St. Thomas School in Leipzig, where he worked until his death. During his working life, Bach wrote an enormous amount of religious choral music, as well as music for organ and harpsichord.

Ludwig van Beethoven (1770-1827)

The German composer Beethoven lived in Vienna, Austria, for most of his life. He was born into a large, musical family and studied music from an early age. In his 20s, it became obvious that he was a talented pianist and composer and by the age of 30 he was a famous pianist. But in about 1796, Beethoven began to go deaf. This made him very frustrated, lonely and difficult to get on with. But he was determined to continue composing music. He carried notebooks around with him in which he jotted down his musical ideas, and wrote some wonderful music even when he was completely deaf. Beethoven is probably best remembered for the energy and power that fills all his music.

Benjamin Britten (1913-1976)

Benjamin Britten was a British composer who is most noted for his skill in bringing character and drama to life through the music of his operas. He began writing music as a child and became a student at the Royal College of Music in London at the age of 17. In 1934 his first important choral work, *A Boy Was Born*, was performed. From 1939 to 1942 he lived in America. In 1945, his most famous opera, *Peter Grimes*, was performed. He founded the English Opera Group and set up the Aldeburgh Festival in his home town of Aldeburgh in Britain. Britten also composed music for children. He wrote *The Young Person's Guide to the Orchestra* in 1945, as an introduction to music for children.

Franz Joseph Haydn (1732-1809)

Haydn was born in Austria, into a poor family. When he was only six, a schoolmaster noticed how musical Haydn was and offered to take over his education. Haydn learned to sing and play various instruments. At 17, Haydn started to teach himself to compose music by studying the work of other composers. Haydn worked as Director of Music to the royal Esterhazy family for 30 years and was known as a gentle man. By 1790 his music was famous throughout Europe. He is best known for his symphonies, of which he composed over 100. He developed the symphony from a short, simple piece of music to a long form for a large orchestra. Haydn is also well known for his operas and other works for voices.

Wolfgang Amadeus Mozart (1756-1791)

Many people consider that the Austrian composer Mozart was the greatest musical genius of all time. He was a child prodigy, and was already composing music and playing the violin and harpsichord with extraordinary talent at the age of five. His parents took Mozart and his sister on tour all round Europe, showing off their brilliance. All the time, Mozart was also writing his own music. Eventually he had to settle down to a job. He worked for a time for the Archbishop of Salzburg as court organist. He composed some dramatic and original music during this time, including his first opera, *Idomeneo*. In spite of many successes, Mozart never had enough money, and he died in comparative poverty.

Sergei Prokofiev (1891-1953)

The Russian composer Prokofiev began studying music at the age of five. He attended the St Petersburg Conservatoire at 13, where his teachers were struck by his musical talent. In 1912 he made his name as a composer and pianist by performing his *1st Piano Concerto* in Moscow. In 1918 he went on a tour of America and in 1920 he went to live in Paris. But he missed Russia, and returned there in 1933. Prokofiev is well-known for his tuneful, highly rhythmic powerful music. He wrote music for operas and ballets as well as concertos and symphonies. His symphonic tale for children, *Peter and the Wolf*, is one of the most popular classical works of the 1900s. Later in his life, he became interested in music for films.

Karlheinz Stockhausen (b.1928)

Stockhausen is a German composer who is well-known for his innovative compositions, which mix electronic and natural sounds. He was born in Cologne and trained at the Music High School in Cologne and then at Cologne University. In 1953, he cofounded an electronic studio called Westdeutscher Rundfunk in Cologne, then from 1954 to 1956 he returned to study at the University of Bonn. Stockhausen is constantly exploring new musical techniques and some of his work leaves space for the performer to improvise, and gives them the opportunity to decide which order to play fragments of music in, and even whether to play them at all. Stockhausen also lectures and writes about experimental music.

Peter Illyich Tchaikovsky (1840-1893)

Tchaikovsky was a Russian composer of melodic music in the romantic style. He was skilled in music from an early age, but began his working life in 1859 as a Clerk in the Ministry of Justice in St. Petersburg. In 1863 he gave up this job to become a composer and by 1873 his talent was becoming widely recognized. From the late 1880s, Tchaikovsky toured as a conductor of his own music. He travelled to Britain and the United States of America. Tchaikovsky drank a glass of unboiled water during an outbreak of cholera. He caught the disease, and was dead within a week. Tchaikovsky is best remembered for his ballets, especially *Swan Lake, The Sleeping Beauty* and *The Nutcracker.*

Glossary of instruments

accordion: a large free-reed instrument with a bellows bag joined by end keyboards with buttons.

anvil: an unusual percussion instrument consisting of steel bars which are hit with a metal striker.

bagpipes: a pipe instrument with reeds sounded with air from a bag, which is inflated by air from the mouth or from bellows.

banjo: a stringed instrument with a long neck and a round body consisting of a parchment skin stretched over a metal hoop.

barrel drum: a drum with a membrane at both ends, played on its side, or with one membrane, stood up to be played.

bass drum: the largest orchestral drum, usually hung on a frame and hit from either side.

bassoon: a double-reed instrument with long, folded tubing.

bell: a hollow percussion instrument struck either from the inside by a clapper or from outside by a striker.

bhaya: an Indian kettledrum. It is the left-hand drum of the tabla.

bodhran: an Irish frame drum struck with a double-headed beater called a pin.

bonnang: two rows of gongs in a straight, low frame from Java.

bongos: a pair of small drums used in Latin American dance bands.

cabaça: a gourd covered with a mesh of beads that rattle when shaken.

castanets: a Spanish percussion instrument. It is two shell-shaped pieces

of wood which are clicked together.

cello: a large stringed instrument, played resting on the floor with the neck leaning against the player's shoulder.

chiming bars: a set of bars of different lengths, hit with small hammers.

clappers: a percussion instrument consisting of two pieces of the same material which are struck together.

clarinet: a single-reed instrument with a system of keys.

clavichord: a small keyboard instrument popular in the 1400s and 1500s.

concertina: a small hand-held instrument with free reeds. Two keyboards with buttons are pulled and pushed to operate a central bellows bag.

congas: a pair of barrel drums, the largest drums used in Latin American dance bands.

cornet: a brass instrument like a small trumpet.

cymbals: dishes of bronze or brass with leather handles. Cymbals are struck or clashed together.

da-daiko: a huge drum used to play Japanese gagaku music.

darbuka: a goblet drum from Islamic countries.

didgeridoo: a long, wooden wind instrument played by Aboriginal people from Australia.

double bass: the largest member of the violin family, it plays the lowest notes.

duct flute: an end-blown flute which has a hole cut into it just below the mouthpiece.

dulcimer: an eastern stringed instrument similar to the zither. The strings are hit with small wooden hammers.

electric guitar: similar to the guitar, but the body is not hollow. Vibrations from the strings are changed into electrical signals.

electric organ: an organ without pipes. Sound is created from electric signals.

eunuch flute: a mirliton found in Europe in the 1700s and 1800s.

finger cymbals: small cymbals played with the finger and thumb.

folk fiddle: a stringed instrument played with a bow.

frame drum: a drum made from one or two membranes stretched over a frame.

French horn: a horn with valves.

friction drum: a drum in which the membrane is made to vibrate by friction of a cord or stick which pierces it.

gambang kayu: a xylophone played in the gamelan orchestra.

gender: a metallophone played in the gamelan orchestra.

glass harmonica: a set of glass bowls played by rubbing a moistened finger round the rims.

glockenspiel: a set of tuned metal bars played with small hammers.

goblet drum: a single-membrane drum with a goblet shape.

gong: a large metal plate hung on a frame and hit with a mallet.

gong ageng: a gong played in the gamelan orchestra.

guitar: a six-stringed instrument played all over the world.

hand bells: a set of small tuned bells played by hand.

harmonica: a western free-reed mouth organ.

harmonium: a free-reed instrument with a long keyboard. The bellows are operated by hand or by foot pedals.

harp: a series of strings stretched from a resonator across a frame and plucked.

harpsichord: a keyboard instrument similar to the piano, but much older.

jalaterang: a set of percussion vessels from India.

jew's harp: a mouth harp with one flexible key.

jingle: a small bell attached to a stick or frame and shaken or worn by a dancer.

kalimba: an mbira played inside a hollow gourd.

kakko: a Japanese drum with two membranes. It rests on a stand and the player strikes both ends.

kazoo: a toy mirliton. A membrane inside it vibrates when the player speaks or sings into the kazoo.

khong wong lek: a set of Thai gongs set in a circular wooden frame.

kettledrum: a drum with a single membrane stretched over a pot-shaped body, often played in pairs.

ko-tsuzumi: an hourglass -shaped drum with two membranes. Used to play music for the Japanese 'No' theatre.

lion roar: a friction drum in which the membrane is made to vibrate with a string.

lithophone: a set of different-sized stones which produce a clear sound when struck.

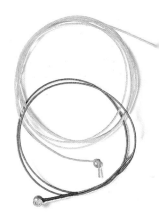

long drum: a tall, thin drum with a single membrane.

lute: a stringed instrument with frets on the fingerboard.

lyre: an ancient stringed instrument with strings stretched between a resonator and a crossbar. The strings are plucked.

maracas: a pair of gourds filled with dry seeds and shaken.

marimba: a Central American xylophone with tubular resonators.

mbira: a set of flexible keys fixed to a wooden block. Also known as the sansa or thumb piano.

melodica: a modern free-reed instrument with a plastic body, a mouthpiece and a small keyboard.

metallophone: a set of tuned chiming bars made from metal.

mirliton: an instrument in which the membrane vibrates to alter the sound made by speaking or singing into it.

mouth harp: an instrument with one flexible key played in the mouth.

musical bow: an instrument which looks like a hunting bow with a single string that is plucked or bowed.

musical saw: a saw held between the knees and played with a bow.

nakers: European drums from the 1100s and 1200s.

naqara: a pair of small kettledrums of Arabic origin.

nose flute: a flute which is sounded with breath from the nose.

oboe: a double-reed instrument developed from the shawm, with a system of keys.

organ: one of the largest wind instruments. An organ has pipes which are operated by air from bellows.

panpipes: a set of different-sized tubes fixed together. Blowing across the top of the pipes makes a musical sound.

pellet drum: a drum with two parts, each with a membrane . The drum is hit with pellets tied on string around the middle of the drum.

piano: the most popular of the keyboard instruments, it can produce a range of loud and soft notes.

piccolo: a smaller version of the orchestral flute, it sounds the higher notes.

pien ch'ing: a set of two rows of L-shaped stones of different sizes.

rattle: a hollow container filled with small objects which rattle when shaken.

recorder: a type of duct flute.

rommelpot: a friction drum which was popular in Europe. The membrane was made to vibrate with a stick.

saron: a metallophone played in the gamelan orchestra.

saxophone: a single-reed instrument, popular in jazz music.

scraper: a rough or ridged object that is rubbed with a rod or the fingers.

serpent: a wooden wind instrument folded into the shape of a snake.

shawm: a folk instrument with a double reed. It is similar to the oboe.

side drum: a small drum with two membranes.

sistrum: a U-shaped rattle with metal discs threaded onto crossbars.

sitar: a stringed instrument from India.

It has main strings, sympathetic strings and drone strings.

snare drum: a side drum with a lower membrane which has strands of wire or nylon stretched over it. These vibrate with the membrane to make a cracking sound.

stamping stick: a hollow tube, closed at one end, which is banged against the ground.

steel pan: a tuned percussion instrument made from an oil drum.

synthesizer: a piece of electrical equipment which makes electrical signals into a range of musical sounds.

tabla: a pair of Indian drums consisting of a larger drum called a bhaya and a smaller one called a tabla.

talking drum: an African drum used to imitate the sound of talking.

tambourine: a small single-membrane drum that often has metal disks attached to the frame.

tiktiri: an instrument made from two or three pipes, each with a single reed and an air reservoir.

timbales: similar to bongos, timbales are played in Latin American dance bands.

timpani: modern orchestral kettledrums.

transverse flute: a side-blown flute. The orchestral flute is a transverse flute with a system of keys.

triangle: a metal bar with a three-cornered shape, struck with a metal beater.

trombone: a brass instrument with a moving piece of tubing called a slide.

trumpet: a brass instrument with a long straight tube or a folded tube. Modern trumpets have a system of valves.

tsuri-daiko: a single-membrane drum used to play Japanese gagaku music.

tuba: a large brass instrument with folded tubing.

tubular bells: a set of tuned metal tubes hung from a frame.

ukulele: a small guitar which originally came from Hawaii.

vessel drum: a bowl-shaped drum with a single membrane.

viol: a six-stringed instrument which is played resting between the player's knees.

viola: a four-stringed instrument similar to the violin but slightly larger.

violin: a four-stringed instrument. Its clear tone and versatility have made it one of the most popular of all western orchestral instruments.

waisted drum: a drum with a pinched-in waist. It can have one or two membranes.

water drum: an American Indian drum made from a metal kettle covered with a single membrane. The drum is filled one-third full of water, which splashes onto the membrane.

whistle: a simple duct flute made from clay, wood, plastic or metal.

wind chimes: small pieces of shell, glass, metal or bamboo hung from strings. They jingle together in the wind.

xylophone: a set of tuned wooden blocks laid out like a keyboard.

zither: a stringed instrument found in many parts of the world. There are several different kinds.

Index

A

Aboriginal people   9, 10, 20, 134–135, 151
accordion 160
Adler, Larry   159
Africa   22, 52, 53, 74, 91, 94–95, 99, 100–101, 105, 142, 151, 154
alto 58, 83
Ancient Egypt   10, 12
Ancient Greece   60, 162
anvil   25, 42
Asia   16, 24, 37, 50, 52, 54, 63, 72–73, 75, 151, 156
Australia   134–135, 146
Austria   79, 83, 87, 141, 145

B

Bach, Johann Sebastian   77, 84, 163, 180
bagpipes   156–157
banjo   64–65
barrel drum   94–96
bass clef   70
bass drum   40, 118–119, 122–123, 127
bassoon   153
baton   80–81
beat   98–99, 109, 114
beater   16, 18, 40, 90, 97–98, 100–101, 117, 119, 123
Beatles, The   73, 85
Beethoven, Ludwig van   93, 179, 180
Belgium   148
bell   34–39
bellows   160–161, 162–163
bendir   124
Berlioz, Hector   119
bhaya   108–109
Blades, James   41
bodhran   102–103
Boehm, Theobald   140
bongos   113
bonnang   17, 30
Booth, William   149
bottleneck   67
bow   52, 54, 56–57
brass instrument   144–149
brass band   148–149, 154
Brazil   113, 130, 167
bridge   55, 56, 74
Britten, Benjamin   41, 119, 181
Brueghel, Pieter   156
bullroarer   167

C

cabaça   12, 45

cantata   84
Caravaggio, Michelangelo Merisi da   62
castanets   11, 40
cello   58–59
change ringing   37
chiming bars   26–28
chin rest   56
China   16, 24, 50, 63, 74, 95, 158
choral music   84–85
chord   71
Chung, Kyung Wah   57
clappers   10–11
clapper bell   37
clarinet   152, 157
clavichord   76
compact disc   170–171
composer   93, 98, 99, 119, 123
concert   172, 173
concertina   161
conductor   29, 80–81
congas   113, 127
cornet   148
counter tenor   83
Cristofori, Bartolomeo   77
crotchet   71
cymbal   14–15, 40

D

da-daiko   114–115
dalang   33
dancing   11, 14, 20, 34–35, 66, 87, 95, 103, 112–113, 124
darbuka   110–111
decibel   92
didgeridoo   134–135, 151
Dixie   154
Dolmetsch, Arnold   138
double bass   51, 58–59
drone string   72
drum set   15, 126–127
drumstick   90, 96–97, 98–99, 103, 112, 114, 116, 121, 127
duct flute   136–137
Dufy, Raoul   122
dulcimer   75
Dylan, Bob   159

E

ear   92
Egypt   144
electric piano   164–165
electric organ   164
Ellington, Duke 155

England 25, 35, 57, 65, 73, 85, 117, 119, 124, 149, 591
Ethiopia 61
eunuch flute 106
Europe 95, 106, 116, 99, 156, 163

F
Fabris, Pietro 55
fanfare 144
Fender, Leo 68
fiddle 54–55
Fiji 142
finger hole 137, 140–141
fingerboard 54, 56, 62, 65, 66
flamenco 11
flute 140–141, 167
Flute Concert at Friedrich the Great's Palace, A 140
Formby, George 65
frame drum 94–95, 102–103, 110
France 106
Franklin, Benjamin 19
free reed 158–161
French horn 147
fret 62–63, 72
friction drum 104–105

G
gagaku 114
gambang kayu 30
gamelan orchestra 17, 27, 30–33
gender 27, 30
Germany 42, 77, 84, 86–87, 163, 179
Ghana 91, 95
Gibson, Orville 68
glass harmonica 19
Glennie, Evelyn 29, 93
glockenspiel 28, 40
goblet drum 94–95, 110–111
gonang 33
gong 16–17, 30, 40
gospel music 85
gourd 12, 13, 23, 26, 106
gramophone 170
guitar 63, 66–69

H
Hals, Frans 104
Hammond, Laurens 164
hand bell 38–39
harmonica 158–159
harmonium 161
harp 61
harpsichord 77

Haydn, Joseph 145, 181
hearing 92–93
Hendrix, Jimi 69
Holland 104
Hungary 78

I
improvisation 71, 72, 154–155
India 37, 52, 71, 74, 95, 114–115, 124, 137, 141, 161, 166, 167
Indonesia 17, 27, 30–33
Inuit 94
Iran 36
Iraq 111
Islam 110–111
Ireland 102–103
Italy 55, 57, 62, 86–87

J
jalaterang 19
Japan 37, 52, 71, 74, 95, 114–115, 124, 136
jazz 23, 59, 69, 85, 99, 127, 154–155
jew's harp 23

K
kakko 114
kalimba 23
kazoo 106
Kenya 142
kettledrum 94–95, 110, 116–117, 118–119
keyboard instrument 76–79, 159, 161, 163, 164–165
khong wong lek 17, 30
ko–tsuzumi 115
Korea 57, 75
koto 74–75

L
Latin America 20
lion roar 105
Liszt, Franz 78
lithophone 24–25
long drum 94–95, 115
lute 62–63
lyre 60–61

M
Magic Flute, The 13, 141
majorette 149
mallet 27, 41
maracas 12
marching 98–99, 122–123
marimba 27, 28

mbira 22–23, 40
measure 98
melodica 159
melody 27, 45, 114
membrane 90–91, 92, 94, 96, 97, 100, 101, 103, 104–105, 106–107, 109, 112, 114, 115, 116, 117, 120, 124
Menuhin, Yehudi 57, 73
Menzel, Adolphe von 138
metallophone 26–28
metronome 174
Mexico 20, 131
microphone 83
military band 122–123, 149
Mingus, Charlie 59
minim 71
mirliton 106
Monteverdi, Claudio 86
Morocco 124
mouth organ 158–159
mouthpiece 136, 144, 147, 150
Mozart, Wolfgang Amadeus 19, 37, 45, 141, 182
muezzin 83
Music at the Customs House at Le Havre 122
musical 87
musical saw 44
Mussorgsky, Modeste Petrovich 146

N
nakers 116
natural trumpet 142–143
New Zealand 86–87
New Guinea 95
Nigeria 94–95, 100–101
'No' theatre 115
North American Indian 12, 54, 95, 103, 112
Northumbrian 'small–pipes' 157
nose flute 167
note 16, 17, 18, 19, 24, 26, 29, 37, 39, 45, 46, 47, 51, 54, 55, 59, 61, 62, 63, 70–71, 75, 76–77, 78–79, 80, 82, 91, 98–99, 117, 133, 135, 137, 139, 141, 145, 150, 157, 158, 174–175
Nutcracker Suite, The 141

O
oboe 152, 157
ocarina 137
octave 29, 71
opera 86–87
oratorio 84
orchestra 15, 28, 40–41, 56, 80–81, 105, 117, 118–119, 139, 144, 146–147, 148, 153
organ 162–163

P
Paganini, Niccolò 57

panpipes 132–133, 141
Parker, Charlie 155
Paul, Les 69
Peasant Dance 156
pedal 69, 77
pellet bell 34–35
pellet drum 107
pelog 33
pentatonic scale 33, 71
percussion 8, 18, 28, 40–41, 90–91, 118–119
Peru 61
Peter and the Wolf 118, 152–153
Philippines 17
piano 77, 78–79
piccolo 141
Pictures at an Exhibition 147
pien ch'ing 24
pitch 29, 33, 39, 54, 75, 117, 133, 137, 140, 144, 147, 150, 175
plectrum 65, 67, 77
plucking 50–51, 52, 64–65
Portugal 63
Prokofiev, Sergei 118, 153, 181
Puccini, Giacomo 87
pulse 98-99

Q
quaver 71

R
raga 72
rattle 12–13
Ravel, Maurice 146
recorder 138–139
recording music 170–171
reed 150–161, 166
reggae 45
resin 56–57, 105
resonator 20, 23, 26, 51, 53, 56, 59, 61, 62, 66, 78, 82, 91
rest 99
Rhine Gold, The 42
rhythm 8–9, 10–11, 12–13, 14, 20, 45, 98–99, 101, 108–109, 112–113, 114, 115, 121, 127
Ring of the Nibelung, The 42
Rite of Spring, The 98
rock music 15, 45, 69, 73, 84, 127, 173
rommelpot 104
Russia 157, 160–161

S
Salvation Army, The 149
sansa 22–23
saron 27, 30
Sax, Adolph 148, 155
saxophone 155
scale 24, 26, 29, 33, 71, 72, 82

Schweninsky, Gemaelde von   42
score   178–179
Scotland 156
Segovia, Andrés   66
semibreve   70
serpent   166
Shankar, Ravi   73
shawm   151, 152, 157
sheng   158
Siberia   103
side drum   119, 120–121, 122
singing   82–87
sistrum   12
sitar   72–73
skiffle   21
slendro   33
snake charmer   166
snare   40, 120–121, 124, 127
Solomon Islands   132
soprano   82
sound wave   90, 92, 131, 150
soundboard   78
Sousa, John Philip   123
South Africa   22
South America   67
Spain   11, 35, 66–67
stave   70
steel pan   44–47
sticks   8–9, 28–29
Stockhausen, Karlheinz   165, 179, 183
stone chimes   24–25
Stradivari, Antonio   57
Stravinsky, Igor   98
string quartet   58
sympathetic string   72
syncopation   99
synthesiser   165

T
tabla   73, 108–109
tala   109
talking drum   100–101
tambourine   119, 124–125
tape   170–171
Tarantella with Posillipo in the Background   55
Tchaikovsky, Peter   141, 183
Te Kanawa, Kiri   86–87
tenor   58–59
tension   91
Three Musicians and a Dancing Girl   34–35, 96
thumb piano   22–23
Tibet   14, 38, 75, 107, 142
tiktiri   166
timbales   113
timpani   40, 116–117, 118–119
tomtom   127
Torres, Antonio   66

treble   58, 82
treble clef   70
triangle   40
trombone   147, 148
trumpet   144–145, 148
Tsar Kolokol bell   36
tsuri–daiko   114
tuba   145, 147, 153, 166
tubular bells   40–41
tuning   16, 18, 33, 47, 51, 80, 117, 175
Turandot   87
Turkey   54
Turn of the Screw, The   41
Tutankhamun   144

U
ukulele   64–65
United States of America   55, 59, 64, 69, 85, 95,
    103, 112, 123, 145, 154–155, 159, 164

V
valve   145, 147, 155
Vaughan Williams, Ralph   159
vessel drum   94–95
vibration   22–23, 26, 50, 51, 52, 54, 57, 62, 68,
    69, 72, 75, 76, 78, 82, 90–91, 92, 96, 106, 120,
    131, 133, 134–135, 143, 144, 150, 152, 158,
    160, 166, 175
viol   56
viola   59
violin   56–58
voice   82–87

W
Wagner, Richard   42, 86
waisted drum   94–95
washboard   21
water drum   112
West Indies   45
whistle   136–137, 140
wind chimes   43
wire brush   96, 127

X
xylophone   26–29, 40

Y
yodelling   83
Yoruba   100–101
Young Person's Guide to the Orchestra, The   119
Young Man Playing a Lute   62

Z
Zambia   105
Zildjian Family   15
Zimbabwe   23
zither   74–75

ACKNOWLEDGEMENTS

The publishers would like to thank the following for permission to reproduce these photographs:

Ace Photo Library for Steel band from Barbados (page 44); string quintet (page 58) and Indian snake charmer (page 166). Axel Poignant Archive for Fijian musicians using stamping sticks (pages 8-9); Aboriginal musician playing wooden clappers (page 10) and Jaguar Playing a Shell Trumpet (page 131). Clive Barda Performing Arts Library for orchestral gong (page 16); Evelyn Glennie (page 29); Benjamin Britten (page 41); orchestral tubular bells (page 41); Kyung Wah Chung (page 57); orchestra (pages 80-81); choir (page 84); Kiri te Kanawa (page 86); scene from Turandot (pages 86-87); musical programme (page 87); Evelyn Glennie (page 93); orchestral timpani (page 118); modern concert flute (page 141) and Karlheinz Stockhausen manuscript (page 179). Bate Collection for Indonesian saron (page 27). Bridgeman Art Library for Three Musicians and a Dancing Girl (pages 34 and 96), by courtesy of the Board of Trustees of the Victoria and Albert Museum; Richard Wagner by Gemaelde von Schweninsky (page 42); Niccolò Paganini (page 57); Young Man Playing a Lute by Caravaggio (page 62); harpsichord (page 77); Persian musicians from A Second Journey Through by James Morier, British Library (pages 110-111); Music at the Customs House at Le Havre by Raoul Dufy, Museé des Beaux-Arts, Le Havre/Giraudon (page 122); A Flute Concert at Friedrich the Great's Palace by Adolphe von Menzel, Staatliche Museen Press, W. Berlin (page 140); Peasant Dance by Pieter Breughel the Elder, Kunsthistoriches Museum, Vienna (page 156); organ case carved by Grinling Gibbons, 17th Century, St. James's Church, Piccadilly, London (page 162) and The Old Hall Manuscript, Polyphonic British Library, London (page 178). The Trustees of the British Museum for Ancient Egyptian sistrum (page 12). Christie's for gramophone (page 170). Collections/Roger Scruton for kettledrums used in Trooping the Colour (page 117). Collections/Brian Shuel for fanfare with long trumpets (page 144) and marching band (page 149). Collections/Anthea Sieveking for girl playing a cello (page 176) and boy playing a guitar (page 177). Colonial Williamsburg Foundation, Virginia, USA for American painting from the 1800s (page 64). Compix/John Leach for Aboriginal didgeridoo player (page 134). Compix/Terry Short for thumb piano and gourd resonator from Zimbabwe (page 23). John Guillaume for Australian tuba player (page 146). The Horniman Museum and Gardens for Ancient Egyptian hand clappers (page 10); South African mbira (page 22); gourd xylophone from Sierra Leone (page 26); jingle from Spain (page 35); lyre (page 61); Portugese fish lute (page 63); Nigerian talking drum (page 101); friction drum from Zambia (page 105) and serpent (page 166). Hutchison Library for Tibetan group playing cymbals (page 14); kulintangan from the Philippines (page 17); khong wong lek from Thailand (page 17); mouth harp players from the Bing Gong Orchestra in Bali (page 23); marimba band from Guatemala (page 27); gamelan orchestra from Bali (page 31); Indonesian puppet threatre (page 32); Tibetan monks playing hand bells (page 38); musical saw player from New York (page 42); Chinese string band (page 50); musical bow from Hitacas (page 53); Peruvian harp player (page 61); Chinese moon guitar player (page 63); Indian print of a sitar player (page 72); Tibetan village orchestra (page 75); South Korean koto player (page 75); Southern Indian drummer (page 90); drummer from Ghana (page 91); dancing drummers from China (page 95); drummers from Rwanda (page 98); talking drummer from Nigeria (page 100); drummer from Siberia (page 103); tabla player (page 108); Da-daiko from Japan (page 115); scene from a Japanese 'No' drama (page 115); musicians from the Mehinack tribe (page 130); natural horn from Kenya (page 142); shawm player from Chad, Africa (page 151); bagpipes from Russia (page 157); Chinese sheng (page 158); accordion at the Moscow folk festival (pages 160-161); harmonium player from India (page 161) and Amazon Indian playing a nose flute (page 167). Mansell Collection for engraving of a rommelpot player by Frans Hals (page 104). James McCormick Performing Arts Library for bassoon player (page 153). The Jeremy Montagu Collection for English lion roar (page 105); darbuka (page 110); European nakers (page 116); naqara (page 116); bass drum (page 123); Moroccan bendir (page 124); Japanese tambourine (page 124) and English tambourine (page 125). Tony Morrison/South American Pictures for samba dancers (page 113). Premier Percussion Ltd for bass drum (page 119). Redferns for modern drum set (page 15); washboard player from an American skiffle band (page 21); Charlie Mingus (page 59); The Gypsy Kings (page 67); Jimi Hendrix (page 69); Ravi Shankar (page 73); gospel choir (page 85); The Chieftains (page 102); drum kit (page 126); trumpet player from New Orleans (page 145); brass section of a modern youth orchestra (pages 146-147); Charlie Parker (page 155); Kathryn Ticknell (page 157); Bob Dylan (page 159); electric Hammond organ (page 164); synthesizer player (page 165); recording studio (page 171); orchestra (page 172) and Live Aid rock concert (page 173). Sefton Photo Library for Andrés Segovia (page 66); soldier marching with a snare drum (page 120) and panpipes player from the Solomon Islands (page 132). Spectrum Colour Library for Russian Kolokol Bell (page 36) and Japanese temple bell (page 37). Tibet Image Bank for long trumpet from Tibet (page 142). Werner Forman Archive for Banquet and Concert (page 136).

The publishers would also like to give special thanks to Carole Mahoney and Danny Staples for their original synopsis and to Emma and Helen Brierley, Merilyn Chambers, Kate Davies, Tim Gray, Mickleburgh Music Shop, Bristol and St. John the Baptist Church, Colerne, for the loan of musical instruments.